HODGES UNIVERSITY

P9-CEO-791

KEEPING
AMERICA
INFORMED

THE U.S. GOVERNMENT PRINTING OFFICE

150 YEARS OF SERVICE TO THE NATION

Hodges University Library

JUN 2 9 2011

U.S. Depository

JOINT COMMITTEE ON PRINTING

111th Congress

CHARLES E. SCHUMER, Senator from New York, *Chairman*
ROBERT A. BRADY, Representative from Pennsylvania, *Vice Chairman*
PATTY MURRAY, Senator from Washington
THOMAS S. UDALL, Senator from New Mexico
ROBERT F. BENNETT, Senator from Utah
SAXBY CHAMBLISS, Senator from Georgia
MICHAEL E. CAPUANO, Representative from Massachusetts
SUSAN A. DAVIS, Representative from California
DANIEL E. LUNGREN, Representative from California
KEVIN McCARTHY, Representative from California

PUBLISHED UNDER THE AUTHORITY OF THE PUBLIC PRINTER OF THE UNITED STATES

WILLIAM J. BOARMAN

UNITED STATES GOVERNMENT PRINTING OFFICE 150TH ANNIVERSARY COMMITTEE

GEORGE D. BARNUM, *GPO Historian*

M. MICHAEL ABRAMSON	KATHERINE D. CLARKE-RADIGAN
JEFFREY S. BROOKE	ANDREW M. SHERMAN
JAMES CAMERON	GARY G. SOMERSET
DEAN A. GARDEI	BETHANN TELFORD
YALANDA JOHNSON	JEFFREY TURNER
GEORGE E. LORD	PAMELA S. WILLIAMS
OKSANA POZDA	EMMA WOJTOWICZ

For sale by the Superintendent of Documents, U.S. Government Printing Office, 732 N. Capitol Street, NW, IDCC Mail Stop, Washington, DC 20401

http://bookstore.gpo.gov | toll free 888.512.1800 | DC area 202.512.1800 | fax 202.512.2250

ISBN 978-0-16-088704-8

TABLE OF CONTENTS

The press that became known as "Press No. 1," bought off the floor of the St. Louis Exposition in 1897. Much of its career was spent printing postal cards, and it remained in service until 1974.

FOREWORD

The U.S. Government Printing Office published its last official history 50 years ago, marking its centennial anniversary. *100 GPO Years 1861–1961* has proven to be a remarkably valuable resource and deserves to stand alone as an enduring contribution to the historical record of this great agency. Instead of trying to improve on it, with the approach of our 150th anniversary we decided to recreate the telling of GPO's story. *Keeping America Informed: The U.S. Government Printing Office: 150 Years of Service to the Nation* recasts our history in a fresh light, with new contributions and emphases, and provides the reader with a greater exposure to GPO's rich photographic record, with many of the images in this book published for the first time.

Most important of all, *Keeping America Informed* describes how the agency has transformed itself through the years by continually adapting to the most efficient technologies available to get its work done. In the ink-on-paper era, this meant moving from handset to machine-set type, from slower to high-speed presses, and from hand to automated bookbinding. These changes enabled GPO to keep up with the demands of a growing Nation and helped keep costs down, and they were significant for their time. Yet they pale by comparison with the transformation that accompanied GPO's incorporation of electronic information technologies, the single most dominant trend at the agency of the past 50 years, and the generator of unprecedented improvements in productivity and hundreds of millions of dollars of taxpayer savings that continue into the present. Today, GPO is fundamentally different from what it was as recently as a generation ago: smaller, leaner, and equipped with digital production capabilities that are the bedrock of the information systems relied upon daily by Congress, Federal agencies, and the public to ensure open and transparent Government in the digital era.

Keeping America Informed is a portrait of the generations of men and women who have worked here as compositors, proofreaders, platemakers, press operators, bookbinders, printing plant workers, librarians, engineering and maintenance staff, accountants, information technology technicians, personnel specialists, police officers, and all the other functions required by GPO. Few Federal agencies can count as their heritage the scope of the work GPO has performed, ranging from the first printing of the Emancipation Proclamation to providing digital access to the Government's publications today. The men and women of GPO are responsible for that heritage. *Keeping America Informed* is a new telling of their story and their enduring achievements.

William J. Boarman, *Public Printer*

Beatrice L. Warde (center) visits GPO in the years immediately after World War II.

CROSSROADS, REFUGE, ARMORY: THIS IS A PRINTING OFFICE

The U.S. Government Printing Office has occupied the same corner of North Capitol Street in Washington, DC, since its founding in 1861. In 1940, after decades of appeals to Congress for more space, GPO opened a new, modern building on the site, replacing a collection of firetrap buildings that had been accumulating for 80 years. In the marble and brass lobby, prominent beside the main elevators, a plaque was placed by the Apprentice Class of 1940, which has been seen by all entering the building ever since:

> *Crossroads of civilization.*
> *Refuge of all the arts against the ravages of time.*
> *Armory of fearless truth against whispering rumor.*
> *Incessant trumpet of trade.*
> *From this place words may fly abroad,*
> *Not to perish on waves of sound,*
> *Not to vary with the writer's hand*
> *But fixed in time,*
> *Having been verified by proof.*
> *Friend, you stand on sacred ground,*
> *This is a Printing Office.*

The words had been written in 1932 by Beatrice L. Warde, an American scholar, writer, and typographer who was publicist for the Monotype Company in England. She is known among designers and typographers for a line of thinking which maintained that type should be a largely transparent medium for the communication of information. Warde designed a broadside for Monotype's introduction of a new typeface called Perpetua, designed by her associate Eric Gill, featuring the "Crossroads of civilization…" text, expressing her beliefs about printing and free societies. The broadside, in the end, proved more popular than the typeface, and a decade later Warde wrote that, "I can say with deep pride that I've seen it framed on the walls of nearly every printing office I have visited. …"[1]

Back in Washington, probably at the urging of GPO Director of Typography Frank Mortimer, the 1940 Apprentice Class had her words cast in bronze, as a sort of blessing and manifesto for the newest building of what had become affectionately known as "the big shop." To Warde, living in Britain as the darkening storm of World War II approached, "…came news from a remote planet (as it then was), the USA, that the inscription was to be cast in bronze and affixed to the wall of the GPO in Washington. There is something about the very words," she continued, "…that sends joyful shivers down any writer's back. …"[2]

The plaque that "sent shivers" down Beatrice Warde's back, and has greeted everyone entering GPO's Building 3 since its opening in 1940.

Seventy years later, at the same location but in the midst of a digital era in which GPO carries out its work using the latest in electronic information technologies, Warde's benedictory words continue to ring true, because they express what we know to be the timeless importance of reproducing and transmitting the written word in our society. Setting down the written word for all to see—whether by applying ink to paper or locking it digitally via public key infrastructure—preserves it, authenticates it, and makes it official, the real thing. This act in turn makes it possible to replicate and disseminate the written word unchanged, providing a common foundation for literacy, education, commerce, the arts, and—perhaps most important of all—the conduct of government in a free society. It was the elemental importance of an informed public to the effective conduct of self-government that prompted James Madison's well-known dictum in an August 4, 1822, letter to W. T. Barry:

A popular Government without popular information, or the means of acquiring it, is but a Prologue to a Farce or a Tragedy, or perhaps both. Knowledge will forever govern ignorance, and a people who mean to be their own Governors, must arm themselves with the power which knowledge gives.

Since its founding 150 years ago, GPO has performed the informing function that Madison spoke of, producing and distributing the documents created by our unique system of government, serving as the "means of acquiring" information for "a people who mean to be their own Governors."

From its earliest days, the function of producing and distributing government documents in America was known as "publick printing." Both before the Revolution and in the early years after the Federal Government was formed, this printing was performed on contract by newspapers and other private printers. By the mid 19th century, however, the high costs, ineffective service, and repeated scandals of contract printing made it clear that the needs of the growing Nation could no longer be satisfied by that system. In its place Congress established the Government Printing Office, and this effort was rewarded almost immediately with a reduction in costs, vastly improved service, and the elimination of scandal. Put to the test early in meeting the emergency demands imposed by the Civil War, the new GPO carried out its work coolly and professionally, counting among its early jobs the printing of the Emancipation Proclamation. In the 150 years that followed, this pattern—economy, efficiency, and prompt and effective service—continued to repeat itself as GPO, quietly and expertly, carried out its mission of keeping America informed.

Most of GPO's past is the story of how the agency moved through successive changes in printing technology to meet the needs and challenges faced by the Nation. By the early twentieth century GPO was acknowledged as the world's largest printing organization, the "big shop." In that capacity the agency supported the needs of the Government through two World Wars and the greatest economic crisis the Nation has ever faced, continuing in that form well into the 1960s, using machine typesetting supported by improving press technology. It was then that the transition to modern information technologies began. Only a year after its centennial, GPO and its congressional oversight panel, the Joint Committee on Printing, began looking for a new way to compose information already captured in Government computer databases. Their initial efforts culminated in 1967 with the installation of the Linotron, a computerized typesetting system developed specifically for GPO's unique needs. From that point forward, the pace of technological change quickened.

Today, GPO's present and future are defined by more than a generation of concentrated investment in digital production and dissemination technologies, an investment that has yielded unprecedented improvements in productivity, capability, product diversity, and savings for the taxpayers. Once an agency of more than 8,000 staff as recently as the 1970s, and employing just 2,200 today—fewer than at any time in the past century—GPO now provides a range of products and services that could only have been dreamed of a generation ago: online databases of congressional and agency documents with state-of-the-art search and retrieval capabilities available to the public without charge, Government publications available as e-Books, passports and smart identification cards with electronic chips carrying biometric data, print products on recycled substrates using vegetable oil-based inks, and a public presence not only on the Web but on Twitter, YouTube, and Facebook. Today, GPO is far more an information agency than a printing office, continuing to carry out Madison's dictum.

At the end of the 20th century, already outfitted with its first Web site, GPO chose for its motto the words "Keeping America Informed," a modern take on the concept of "publick printing," a notion that has been at the center of its existence from the first day. GPO has done its job using continually evolving and improving technology placed in the hands of thousands of skilled men and women who have, in turn, produced and delivered documents of every description for Congress, Federal agencies, and the public.

The story of GPO's 150 years is a story of the Republic's need for the written word, the machines and technologies that have been used to fulfill that need, and the thousands of dedicated men and women of the Government Printing Office who have risen to the challenge of producing and distributing the documents required by our Federal Government. It is the story of what we do, how we do it, and who we are. It is the story of humble documents and hallowed, sometimes beautiful and sometimes utterly plain. It is the story of remarkable machines that flourished, faded, and were succeeded by newer and better technologies. And it is the story of people, careers, and lives here on our own corner of Washington, DC, reaching across the country, keeping America informed for 150 years. ✍

1861-1880

"PUBLICK PRINTING" AND THE FOUNDING OF GPO

In the more than 80 years before the establishment of the Government Printing Office, the concept of printing and distributing the official documents of the government had been well established in the United States. However, the ways in which those functions were carried out left much to be desired. Indeed, at least one observer has noted, "the National Government was not well served by" those arrangements.[3] Work often was performed sporadically and there are many examples of incomplete or nonexistent records from the early Congresses. Worse, the original systems of Government printing were costly and frequently subject to corruption and public scandal. The story of "publick" printing and the founding and early years of GPO is a story of how Congress struggled with different systems of keeping America informed, and how GPO—once it began operations—contributed to that responsibility in an era of civil war that included the production of one of the most celebrated documents in American history—the Emancipation Proclamation.

The Colonial Era

Printing first appeared in British America in 1639 when a printing press was imported from England and installed at Harvard College in Cambridge, Massachusetts. The colonists who arrived in America brought with them a tradition of printing and literacy, and with the growth of the colonies, newspaper printing became an important source of news and information. A chief source of revenue for these struggling early papers was official "crown," or "publick," printing—legislative and other government documents—which newspapers were best equipped to perform since they had the equipment, paper, and the necessary skilled labor.

One of those "publick" printers—and there were many, with most colonies frequently employing several—was Benjamin Franklin. Franklin was an enterprising businessman who produced official documents for Pennsylvania, Delaware, Maryland, and New Jersey. His brother James worked in a similar capacity for Massachusetts and Rhode Island. Other "publick" printers included many now famous names, such as John Peter Zenger and William and Thomas Bradford. "Publick" printers first set type for the Declaration of Independence. They worked on behalf of the delegates to the new state legislatures and later the Philadelphia Convention of 1787, setting the type for the new Constitution. Many of them also printed the newspaper-based debates on ratification of the Constitution that were later collected as the *Federalist Papers*.

Along with printing, the American colonists brought with them from England the Enlightenment notion that the people have a right to know about the laws and proceedings of their Government, a notion articulated by John Milton in his essay *Areopagitica*, an argument against censorship and the licensing of printing, published in 1644: "Give me the liberty to know, to utter, and to argue freely according to conscience, above all liberties. ..." The practice of printing the acts of Parliament had been established in England, forming the precedent for "publick

PHILADELPHIA.

In CONGRESS, Thursday, September 22, 1774.

RESOLVED,

THAT the Congress request the Merchants and Others, in the several Colonies, not to send to Great Britain any Orders for Goods, and to direct the execution of all Orders already sent, to be delayed or suspended, until the sense of the Congress, on the means to be taken for the preservation of the Liberties of *America*, is made public.

An Extract from the Minutes,

CHARLES THOMSON, *Sec.*

Printed by *W.* and *T. BRADFORD.*

The first official document produced by the government of what would become the United States of America is today known simply as "Government Document No. 1." Dated September 22, 1774, the document was a 6¾" by 4¼" broadside, or public notice, issued by the First Continental Congress and printed in Philadelphia, where the Congress was meeting. William and Thomas Bradford, who provided all printing for the Continental Congress from 1774 to 1776, printed it. Signed by Charles Thomson, Secretary, it called for the non-importation of British goods "until the sense of Congress, on the means to be taken for preservation of the Liberties of America, is made public."[4]

---

printing" in the New World. By the time of the Revolution, the concept of public access to government information was widespread. The 1776 Pennsylvania Constitution, for example, included the phrase: "The printing presses shall be free to every person who undertakes to examine the proceedings of the legislature, or any part of government."[5]

The concept of public access was adopted by the new national government. The Continental Congress passed a resolution "…that the Journals…be printed…weekly." The Articles of Confederation said, "The Congress of the United States…shall publish the journal of their proceedings monthly. …" During the Constitutional Convention, the issue of public access to government information came up again. Patrick Henry of Virginia said, "The liberties of a people never were, nor ever will be, secure, when the transactions of their rulers may be concealed from them. …" James Wilson of Pennsylvania agreed, saying, "The people have a right to know what their agents are doing or have done, and it should not be in the option of the legislature to conceal their proceedings." Article I, section 5, of the Constitution established the requirement that "Each House shall keep a Journal of its Proceedings, and from time to time publish the same. …"[6]

Printing for the Early Congresses

Soon after the First Congress organized in early 1789, a recommendation was made in the House of Representatives that proposals be invited for "printing the laws and other proceedings." By May, printers' petitions flowed in asking to be employed in the printing for Congress. The House Journal for the first and second sessions of the First Congress was printed by New York printers Francis Childs and John Swaine, and the Senate work was done by John Fenno. The Secretary of the Senate and the Clerk of the House were directed by a joint committee to have printed 600 copies of the acts of Congress and 700 copies of the journals. When Congress moved to Philadelphia in 1790, Childs & Swaine and Fenno moved with them, joined by Philadelphian Samuel H. Smith. Together these firms produced the bulk of congressional printing from 1793 to 1800. The expense of public printing for Congress was not inconsiderable. An act of 1794 allocated $10,000 for the expenses of firewood, stationery, and printing work, and all other contingent expenses of the two houses of Congress.

When Congress moved to the new capital in Washington in 1800, printers followed and set up shop in the raw wilderness city. President Thomas Jefferson encouraged Smith to move from Philadelphia, and

The Congressional Serial Set

In addition to devising a system for printing documents, Congress developed a system for organizing its documents for posterity. Beginning in 1817, serial numbers were assigned to Senate and House documents, congressional committee reports, Presidential and other executive publications, treaty materials, and selected reports of nongovernmental organizations. This numbering scheme proved to be an orderly and convenient way of identifying and preserving the documents and reports issued by Congress. Now known as the *U.S. Congressional Serial Set*, these publications have been produced continuously since that time. In the words of historian Dee Brown, it "contains almost everything about the American experience…our wars, our peacetime works, our explorations and inventions…If we lost everything else in print, except our documents, we would still have a splendid record and a memory of our past experience."[7]

The Serial Set contains innumerable unique and unusual items. One of these is the first published work of the artist James McNeil Whistler, who as a young man worked briefly as an engraver in the cartographic section of the U.S. Coast Survey. One copper plate etching he produced

was published in the *Report of the Coast Survey for 1854*… It contains a map and view of Anacapa Island in California. The map itself is credited to Capt. L.W. Stevens, USN. The accompanying view of the rocky shoreline in the Santa Barbara Channel at the bottom of the page carries a credit to Whistler in its lower right corner. The National Archives described Whistler's drawing: "After he completed his etching in the approved style, he thought it looked dull. Therefore, he added two flocks of gulls sailing gracefully over the rocky headland."[8]

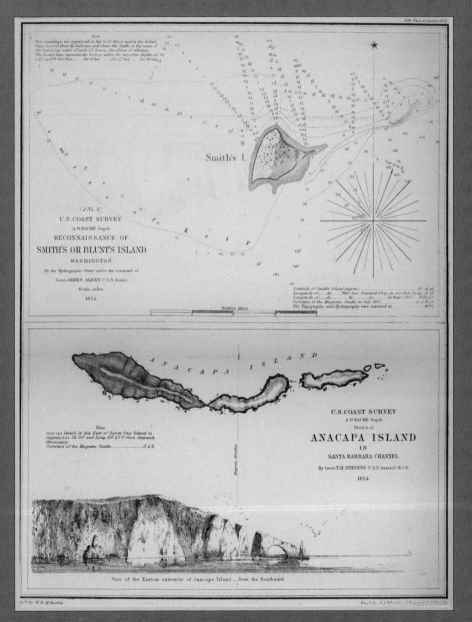

by 1801 he was printing reports of congressional debates in his *National Intelligencer* three times a week. Its stenographers took notes in Congress and later asked speakers to review them prior to publication. Delay and inaccuracy were common. In December 1801, a proposal was made by Virginia Representative John Randolph to appoint a single printer to provide for the "faithful and prompt execution" of printing for the House. The measure was defeated, however, and the work was left to enterprising local printers.

Not until 1818 was another effort made to address the shortcomings of local printing. Congress appointed a joint committee to "consider and report whether any further provisions of law are necessary to insure dispatch, accuracy, and neatness in printing done for the two houses of Congress." In 1819, the committee issued a report asking that Congress consider

> the establishment of a national printing office (with a bindery and stationery annexed) which should execute the work of Congress while in session and that of the various Departments of Government during the recess, and should do all the binding, and furnish all the stationery for the Departments, as well as for Congress…The Committee are of the opinion that such an establishment, under the superintendence of a man of activity, integrity, and discretion, would be likely to produce promptitude, uniformity, accuracy, and elegance in the execution of public printing. …

The time for reform had not yet arrived, however, and instead of a Government Printing Office and a Public Printer, a hasty resolution of March 2, 1819, provided that the House and Senate should elect their own printers, instruct how the work should be done, and say what price should be paid. Thus began the swing of the pendulum between Congress's use of fixed rates and low-bid contracting for printing that would, in their many inadequacies, set the stage for the eventual creation of the Government Printing Office.

Printing and Profits

The practice of electing House and Senate printers persisted for forty years, and throughout this period there was intense rivalry for these posi-

tions. These printers included names now chiefly remembered for their connection with Government printing: Gales & Seaton, Duff Green, Blair & Rives, Thomas Allen, Peter Force, and Ritchie & Heiss. The reason for the rivalry was clear: The volume of work and relatively stable demand for their services made many of these firms prosperous and their proprietors well-to-do. Their prosperity stemmed from advances in printing technology that made it increasingly profitable to produce public printing under Congress's fixed rate system. Improved presses enabled the production of more work with less labor, yet the fixed rates set by Congress were based on older, slower processes. Within five years of securing congressional work, for example, one such firm—Blair & Rives—purchased their rented premises, bought handsome houses (including the one now used as the President's guest house, Blair House), and acquired country estates.

To deal with the continuing problem of its printing, in 1840 the House appointed a Select Committee on Public Printing and asked it to report on prices considered just and reasonable, the propriety of separating Government printing from newspaper publishing, and the practicality of a national printing office. The investigation resulted in a bill directing "that there shall be erected on suitable spot in the city of Washington, to be selected by the President of the United States, a building of brick, suitable and convenient for a printing office in which all the printing for Congress, and for the Executive Departments, and for the Post Office Department, shall be performed." Once again, the bill did not pass, and Congress continued with its system of fixed rates. Another congressional printing study was made in 1842, again without result.

Between 1840 and 1846, Congress passed a series of laws providing for competitive contract printing for various Government departments and the Supreme Court, and then moved to implement this method for its own printing. The House Select Committee submitted a joint resolution of August 3, 1846, directing advertisements in local newspapers at the beginning of the last session of each Congress, requesting sealed bids for Senate and House printing in the coming Congress. The 1846 joint resolution also established the Joint Committee on Printing to manage the requirements of the House and Senate, with the authority to adopt measures "deemed necessary to remedy neglect, delay, or waste" in Government printing. The Committee, known familiarly as the JCP, continues to operate to this day. The first printers to win a contract under the new system were Charles van Benthuysen and Cornelius Wendell. Wendell later would become a prominent name in the origin of the Government Printing Office.

The contract system of printing established in 1846, unfortunately, "proved the most expensive of any tried up to this time, and perhaps the most unsatisfactory." As one observer has noted:

> While the underlying intent of the new law was to promote economy and prevent fraud by opening the printing function to a larger field of entrepreneurs… contracts were executed without care, and exorbitant printing costs resulted. Plates for Government documents were destroyed after a first publication run and had to be redrawn, at considerable expense, if additional copies of an item were ordered. Engravings produced for one congressional chamber and later sought by the other House were priced as originals.[9]

As a result, printing costs for the Government during the period from 1846–1852 amounted to $3,462,655.12, nearly as much as had been expended in the preceding 35 years combined, and at a moment when technology was constantly reducing the cost of printing.

Congress sought to address the problem of costs in an act of August 25, 1852, when it returned to the earlier practice of the two chambers electing their own printers under rates fixed by law. This act also provided for a Superintendent of Public Printing to supervise the printers for the House and Senate, supplementing the oversight of the Joint Committee on Printing. The Superintendent was to be "a practical printer versed in the various branches of printing and bookbinding, and shall not be interested, directly or indirectly, in any contract for printing for Congress or for any department or bureau of the Government of the United States." John T. Towers, of Washington, DC, was selected by President Millard Fillmore to serve as the first Superintendent. After his term as Superintendent, he went on to serve as mayor of Washington.

The act of 1852 proved a failure, however. One difficulty was the lack of an office with proper facilities for executing the printing promptly and uniformly. The demands of the Government had increased to such an extent that by 1856 no single printing office in Washington was capable of handling all the printing required, with the result that layouts, fonts, and other printing details varied from job to job. The other and greater difficulty was that renewal of the fixed rate system for printing generated enormous profits for those performing the work both for Congress and the executive agencies. A portion of the profits were converted into political contributions, which were given in exchange for preference in the award of printing contracts.

> Politicians who had no practical knowledge of printing succeeded in securing the place of printer, and farmed out the work to practical printers at a percentage of the receipts. The dominant party elected the printer with a positive understanding that he would devote specified sums out of his profits for partisan purposes… In some cases six times a fair rate was paid for certain jobs and the plunder thus secured was systematically distributed for partisan purposes…[10]

Three more Superintendents were selected between 1854 and 1859: A.G. Seaman (1853), General George W. Bowman (1857), and John Heart (1859). Until 1860, the two chambers continued to elect printers who worked under the oversight of the Superintendents. By the close of the 1850s, however, reliance on newspapers and other printers for congressional and executive agency work was less and less attractive. Public outcry over scandals, fraud, and corruption lead to major congressional investigations in 1858 and 1860, with one investigation in 1860 disclosing overcharges to the Government of $750,000.

GPO is Born

Congressional reaction to this chaos produced a reform bill in 1860, sponsored by Ohio Representative John Addison Gurley, a former newspaperman and chairman of the Select Committee on Public Printing. House Resolution 22 (36th Congress) called for the establishment of a government printing office and passed on May 31, 1860, after a vigorous debate. The Senate concurred on June 16, and a further Joint Resolution (No. 25) was passed on June 23. It directed the Superintendent of Public Printing "to have executed the printing and binding authorized by the Senate and House of Representatives, the executive and judicial departments, and the Court of Claims," and authorized him to "contract for the erection

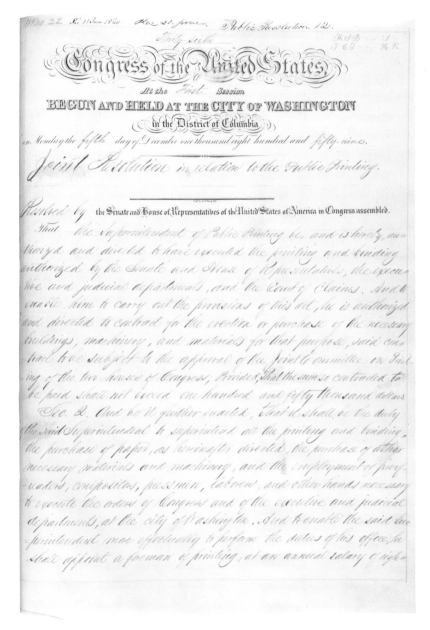

The first page of the Congressional Joint Resolution that created GPO, June 1860.

Above: *The area north of the Capitol about 1830. The train crosses Tiber Creek a little to the south of the present day site of GPO, which stretches beyond the first car behind the locomotive.* (Library of Congress)
Right: *Cornelius Wendell (1811–1870), printer, entrepreneur, and later Superintendent of Pubic Printing.*

or purchase of the necessary buildings, machinery, and materials for that purpose." Joint Resolution 25 stipulated that the new office would begin its working life on March 4, 1861, the first day of the new Presidential administration.

To carry out this act, then Superintendent Heart moved swiftly to negotiate the purchase of the printing establishment built in 1857 by Cornelius Wendell at the corner of H and North Capitol Streets in the northwest quadrant of the District. The area was still largely farmland to the north and east, and was cut through by the B&O railroad, whose terminal was at First Street and New Jersey Avenue. Tiber Creek, which ran alongside the property, regularly overflowed, creating swampland and puddles, and the neighborhood was well known as "Swampoodle."

Wendell was closely connected with the printing work for both chambers in the 1850s, and at various times during the period leading to GPO's creation had been responsible for most Government printing. He had been House Printer in 1856, and throughout the last period of private enterprise printing was often the subcontractor who actually put documents to press for many of the elected and appointed printers of the House and Senate. Wendell had profited by his years of congressional work and had built a plant capable of accommodating the large and growing demands of the Government. *The Printer*, in an illustrated article in 1858, reported that, "Others who had in turn been [Superintendent] had either been interested in the newspaper offices of the metropolis or had engaged them to do the work required, but Mr. Wendell determined to have a Public Printing Office worthy of the Great Republic."[11] Following the passage of Joint Resolution 25, an independent appraiser valued the Wendell plant, including machinery, at $146,545. A contract for the purchase by the Government for $135,000 was signed on December 1, 1860, and approved by Congress on December 12.

John B. Ellis, in his *Sights and Secrets of the National Capitol*, described the Wendell plant and its section of Washington a few years after its acquisition by the Government:

> If you stand on Capitol Hill, at the top of the high flight of stairs leading into the Senate, and look straight north you will see the Government Printing Office…the settled quarter of the city lies west of and behind the printing office. Making a straight way across Tiber Creek, which you will cross by stepping stones deposited in its basin, and taking a footpath across lots where geese and pigs browse upon plentiful barrenness, you will reach the printing house…and hear the hum of its machinery as you take in coup d'oeil.[12]

The approaching visitor first caught sight of the tall chimney of GPO's engine house and the main building, designed by Architect of the Capitol Edward Clark in 1856, and opened on November 16, 1857. It was the largest printing office in the city, and one of the largest and most complete in the Nation. In addition to the imposing main building with its cupola and eagle, a machine shop, stable, paper storehouse, and various other storehouses and sheds stood on the site.

The plant employed about 350 workers, including a large number of women as both bindery workers and press feeders. It was equipped with 23 Adams bed-and-platen presses and three Napier cylinder presses, all steam-driven. The presses were supplied with forms from 93 double composing stands and 349 pairs of cases with more than 25 tons of foundry type. Composition, proofreading, and pressrooms occupied the first and second

Above: *Congress bought this brick building and all its machinery and equipment from Cornelius Wendell to serve as the Government Printing Office in 1861. It faced H Street at the corner of North Capitol Street.* Right: *John Dougherty Defrees (1810-1882), President Lincoln's Superintendent of Public Printing.*

View from the roof of the Senate side of the Capitol, June 1861. The building in the middle distance beyond the flagstaff is GPO, the smokestack of the engine house is visible in the right foreground. (Library of Congress)

The Binding Division in the 1860s.

The Composing Division in the 1870s.

floors, while the upper floors were devoted to bindery operations, including ruling of blank forms and blank books, one of the office's major products.

To guide the new operation, President Abraham Lincoln appointed John Dougherty Defrees, effective March 23, 1861. Born in Tennessee in 1810, Defrees was the son of a father hostile to slavery, who moved the family to Ohio in 1818. The young Defrees was apprenticed to a printer in 1814, began as a journeyman at 17, and later worked in Cincinnati and Louisville, Kentucky. At 21, he established a newspaper in South Bend, Indiana, and in 1846 he purchased the *Indiana State Journal* in Indianapolis. He was to serve as head of GPO three times: 1861–66, 1867–69, and 1877–82.

Defrees was eager to demonstrate the value of the new GPO. In his first annual report, he said "a saving of least $60,000 has been effected [over the fixed charges in the 1852 act]." By his second annual report, he showed a savings of $205,506, and in his third annual report Defrees was able to show a total saving in printing costs of $583,935. He wrote, "The character of the printing and binding, in material and workmanship, is superior to that furnished under any system which has preceded the present; and the experiment of the Government doing its own work, both as regards its quality and the economy of its cost, may be regarded as completely successful."

Most of the new GPO's employees were union members, belonging either to the Columbia Typographical Society as compositors and pressmen, or to the bookbinders' union. Founded in 1815, the Columbia Typographical Society was America's first union, with members working throughout the Washington, DC, area, including throughout the newspapers and other printshops that performed congressional work in the years before GPO was established. Renamed the Columbia Typographical Union (CTU) in 1867, it was an early supporter of the 8-hour work day as well as the creation of GPO. The union supported the admission of black members and women into its ranks sooner than its counterparts in other craft unions and well before such diversity was common in the national workforce.[13] The tradition of labor representation in GPO's workforce continues to this day, including CTU, Local 101.

Columbia Typographical Union, Chapel 1, at GPO, probably about 1890. The present Local 101 is a direct descendant.

GPO During the Civil War

Defrees and the new GPO began work in Washington at a tumultuous time. In his 1863 Annual Report, Defrees said, "During the last year the amount of printing required by the Government…has been very great, much greater than at any former period. The necessity for this increase, it is needless to say, is to be found in the existing condition of the country." The pattern of wartime as catalyst for GPO growth was set early and continued through much of the next century.

A Civil War camp in Washington, DC.

Soldiers mustered in front of the Senate side of the Capitol. (Library of Congress)

The war touched many at GPO personally. In 1863, President Lincoln responded to a request from Defrees to visit GPO on October 24. In a letter, Defrees later recounted an incident from the visit:

> A poor girl in the employment of the GPO had a brother impressed into the rebel service, and was taken prisoner by our forces. He desired to take the oath of allegiance, and to be liberated. She sought an interview with the President who wrote the note asking me to inquire into the facts, which I did, and the young man was liberated on the President's order.

Defrees was active in the liberal wing of the Whig Party and was a delegate to the Whig and, later, National Republican Conventions of 1848, 1852, and 1856. A skillful and passionate politician, Defrees was an ardent supporter of Lincoln and antislavery causes. For the Indiana State Journal he had hired such antislavery writers as Henry Ward Beecher. As Public

Printer, he carried this activism into office. On February 7, 1864, he sent a letter of advice to President Lincoln. It asked, "…why not send a message to Congress recommending the passage of a joint resolution proposing an amendment to the Constitution forever prohibiting slavery in the States and territories?" Lincoln's prompt reply of February 8 said, "Our own friends have this under consideration now, and will do as much without a Message as with it."

GPO contributed more than just printing to the war effort. In 1864, Washington, DC, came under threat of invasion as General Jubal A. Early's Confederate forces approached from the northwest to within five miles of the Capital. A number of GPO employees were a part of what was known as the Interior Department Regiment, organized to help protect the city. Printers and press operators made up Company F and bindery workers comprised Company G. Hours were set aside for drill and instruction and GPO was guarded at night. With the imminent threat of Early's raid, Company F was mustered and took up defensive positions across the Anacostia, probably at Fort Stanton. When reinforcements from General Grant's forces at Petersburg helped repulse the attack at Fort Stevens in upper northwest Washington, GPO's companies returned to work in Swampoodle.

The Postwar Period

The original Wendell building had been expanded in 1865 with a four-story addition at the west end of the main building. Another four-story addition fronting on North Capitol Street was added in 1871. In 1879, a fireproof building was added south of the main building, and in 1880–81, GPO purchased a lot on H Street and put up a stable and a second fireproof extension west of the North Capitol Street section.

Driving these expansions were the ongoing need for adequate space and concerns over the safety of workers. As demand grew, cramped conditions and accidents not only injured a skilled workforce, but slowed down production and increased overall cost. A typical concern was voiced by Superintendent Clapp in his 1869 Annual Report:

> The building now occupied by the Government Printing Office has, under the increase of its business, become insufficient for its proper accommodation. Indeed it is impossible

The Emancipation Proclamation

In 1862, GPO undertook the most significant printing job of its day or of any GPO since then: the production of President Lincoln's Emancipation Proclamation.

After drafting a "Preliminary Proclamation" and previewing it with Secretary of State William Seward and Secretary of the Navy Gideon Welles on July 13, Lincoln raised the matter again in a Cabinet meeting on July 22, to mixed reaction. But his mind was already made up, and he brought the document before the Cabinet again on September 22, five days after the Union army turned back the Confederate army's advance into the North at the Battle of Antietam. Historian John Hope Franklin describes what happened next:

The historic meeting of the Cabinet was hardly over on September 22, 1862, before the printing and distribution of the preliminary Proclamation had begun. That afternoon and evening the employees of the Government Printing Office worked late and prepared copies for distribution to the press and government agencies. Seward…ordered copies that were to go, along with a circular, to the numerous diplomatic posts of the United States in foreign countries. For the War Department, fifteen thousand copies of General Orders, number 139, dated September 24, 1862, and including the Proclamation, were printed and readied for distribution among the various military commanders and their troops. The Preliminary Proclamation had been long coming. But once the decision was made and the document signed, there was no delay in presenting it to the world.[14]

The Preliminary Proclamation was issued "in general orders format, as an order from the Commander-in-Chief to the armed forces. Because he had direct control over the Army, the President thus made it unnecessary to go through Congress to activate the Proclamation."[15] The printed version of the Preliminary Proclamation was later marked for correction, and the final Emancipation Proclamation, issued January 3, 1863, bore those corrections. Well aware of its significance, Public Printer Defrees closely followed the progress of the Proclamation, writing in December 1862 to President Lincoln's secretary, John G. Nicolay, "Only a few events stand out prominently on the page of the history of each century…The proposed proclamation of the President will be that one of this century."[16]

The first printing of the Emancipation Proclamation with corrections noted in pencil (perhaps from GPO proofreaders) that were incorporated into the Proclamation as it was issued on January 3, 1863. (Library of Congress)

now to crowd within its walls sufficient machinery and operatives to keep up with the demands made upon its resources, especially in the binding department. The buildings now used for storing large quantities of paper necessarily kept on hand are insufficient, inconvenient, unsuitable, and unsafe, and should be discontinued in their use for that purpose.

Supporting arguments were marshaled from Architect of the Capitol Clark. Clark toured GPO in 1870 and observed in a letter that, "Prudence demands that measures should be taken to procure additional capacity, and that all heavy loads possible should be placed on the ground floor." In 1878 Clark provided a plan for outside fire escapes, for which Congress appropriated $3,000. These were "…of brick and iron, very substantial, so that, should a fire occur…they would afford additional and ample means of escape." In 1880, fire extinguishers, which had been invented in the early 19th century, were acquired and GPO workers were instructed in their use.

Almon M. Clapp (1811–1899), the first appointee to hold the title Public Printer.

During this period the practice of having a Presidential appointee at GPO's helm was permanently established. The first heads of GPO were Presidential appointees with the title Superintendent of Public Printing. Cornelius Wendell, appointed by President Andrew Johnson to succeed Superintendent Defrees in September 1866, served to February 1867. During his brief term, he averted a major printer's strike and instituted an eight-hour workday and a six-day week. Meanwhile, a Congress at odds with President Johnson decided to elect GPO's head and make him an officer of the Senate, with the title Congressional Printer. The Senate elected John Defrees, who served from March 1867 to April 1869. In this second term at GPO, Defrees secured for the Office the printing and binding work of the Patent Office and the Commissioner of Customs.

Defrees was followed by Almon M. Clapp, a Connecticut native with many years of printing experience, who was elected in April 1869 as

Superintendent Defrees' order establishing an 8-hour workday on Saturdays, the first step toward the 40-hour workweek.

(The order reads: You will please direct that, hereafter, the work in this office will end on Saturdays at 4 o'clock P.M.

I am induced to establish this rule because I believe that men who labor faithfully during the week ten hours per day need more recreation at the end of the week than they now receive, and, because that, if the rule is adopted, they will so appreciate it that the Government will really lose nothing by its operation.

Yours truly, John D. Defrees, Supt. Pub. Printing)

Congressional Printer. Clapp was to see Congress change its mind about his title after the departure of President Johnson, and in July 1876, repeal the earlier legislation and specify a Presidential appointment for GPO's top official, with the advice and consent of the Senate. The appointee's title became Public Printer, harking back to the title held by printers of government documents in the pre-Revolutionary War era. In August 1876, President Ulysses S. Grant made Clapp the first Public Printer. He was followed, as he had been preceded, by Defrees, who was appointed by President Rutherford Hayes in June 1877 and served until April 1882. The post has been filled by Presidential appointees with the consent of the Senate ever since.

It was also during this period that the first congressional investigation of the new GPO was launched, conducted by the Joint Committee on Printing. The Committee looked into allegations of cronyism in the distribution of composing work and favoritism in appointments to the agency, including a charge that GPO had hired "a man who left this city at the outbreak of the rebellion and served three years in the rebel army." After a thorough review, the JCP reported in 1870 that while "your committee do [sic] not pretend to say the management of the GPO by the present Congressional Printer [Almon Clapp] has been perfect. …The allegations…are not sustained by the evidence, and the services of the Congressional Printer appear to have been faithful, and in results valuable to the Government." The JCP's role in overseeing GPO was established by this investigation and has continued to this day.

The *Congressional Record*

Another development in this period had a lasting impact on GPO's operation and reputation, and is emblematic of the ultimate success of the Office's creation and expansion: the creation of the *Congressional Record*. The publication of Congress' proceedings was exempt from the legislative action that created GPO in 1860, and remained in the hands of contractor printers who published congressional newspapers of various kinds using transcripts obtained by sending reporters into the chambers. One of these, the *Congressional Globe*, had begun reporting debates in 1831 as a semiweekly owned by Francis Preston Blair, a Kentucky native and member of President Andrew Jackson's "Kitchen Cabinet." Blair took a fellow Kentuckian, John C. Rives, as partner, and the *Globe* became a weekly in 1833. It persisted with varying ownership until the 1870s, and was subject to criticism from rival printers. In 1871, the contract was set to be rebid and controversy ensued over the charges for the preceding several years. The contract was awarded to F&J Rives and Bailey for one year, at the excessive cost of $400,000, compared with the previous cumulative cost of $744,117 for the entire period 1861–1871.

In response, the 42nd Congress sent invitations to bid on a proposed six-year contract to printers in nine cities nationwide, including the Congressional Printer. After evaluating the bids, Congress passed a measure that said, in part, "…until a contract is made, the debates shall be printed by the Congressional Printer under the Joint Committee on Printing on the part of the Senate." In the end, GPO's estimate of

The last issue of the Congressional Globe, 1873. (Law Library of Congress)

The premiere issue of the Congressional Record, March 4, 1863. A "great improvement" according to the New York Times.

"…$150 for each and every 1,000 ems, printer's measurement…" was accepted in both chambers, by a wide majority, giving GPO responsibility for this document. The *New York Times* reported on March 4, 1873, that, "after the Congressional Printer shall have completed arrangements to do the work, it is hardly probable that any effort to get the work into the hands of private printers can succeed."

The JCP provided the name of the new publication, to be published daily when Congress was in session, and the *Congressional Record* first appeared on March 5, 1873. Congressional Printer Clapp noted that, "The change in the form and style of this publication from that previously followed by the *Globe* was induced by a desire to secure comeliness, convenience, and economy for the work; and I am gratified in the assur-ance that it meets the hearty approval of the Senate and the House of Representatives. …" The first-year charges were $126,000, a substantial saving over the contract with Rives & Bailey. Clapp continued, "The facilities of the office are so extensive that prompt publication of the pro-ceedings and debates of any day's session, no matter how extensive or volu-minous, will be assured by the following morning without peradventure." Although in 1873 the *Record*, like all other GPO documents, was entirely set by hand (and would be until 1904), the standard of overnight produc-tion was established. The *Record* has been a pillar of GPO's work ever since. In subsequent years, the JCP established the laws and rules under which the *Record* is to be produced, and the committee today remains the official publisher of the *Record* by law. ❧

THE OFFICIAL RECORDS OF THE WAR OF THE REBELLION

Closing out GPO's early years was the assignment to produce one of the most historically significant jobs ever, *The War of the Rebellion: A Compilation of the Official Records of the Union and Confederate Armies*. Authorized by Congress in 1874 and widely acknowledged as the most extensive collection of primary documents relating to the Civil War ever produced, the *OWR*, as it has become known in Civil War bibliographies, was one of the largest single printing jobs ever undertaken by GPO. Public Printer Defrees, by then serving his third and final term at GPO's helm, initially estimated the work would make 96 volumes of 10,050 copies each, totaling 964,800 volumes. As finally published, the *OWR* consists of more than 138,000 pages with more than 1,000 maps and diagrams assembled in 128 volumes. The Office of War Records compiled the history and composition began at GPO in 1880. The work was not completed until the early years of the new century. By then, historic changes in printing technology were fundamentally altering the way GPO carried out its mission.

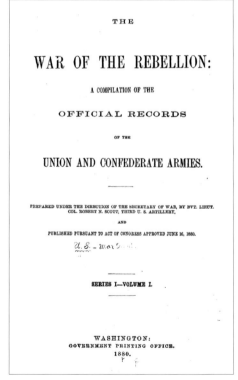

THE

WAR OF THE REBELLION:

A COMPILATION OF THE

OFFICIAL RECORDS

OF THE

UNION AND CONFEDERATE ARMIES.

PREPARED UNDER THE DIRECTION OF THE SECRETARY OF WAR, BY BVT. LIEUT. COL. ROBERT N. SCOTT, THIRD U. S. ARTILLERY,

AND

PUBLISHED PURSUANT TO ACT OF CONGRESS APPROVED JUNE 16, 1880.

SERIES I—VOLUME I.

WASHINGTON:
GOVERNMENT PRINTING OFFICE.
1880.

(Cornell University Libraries)

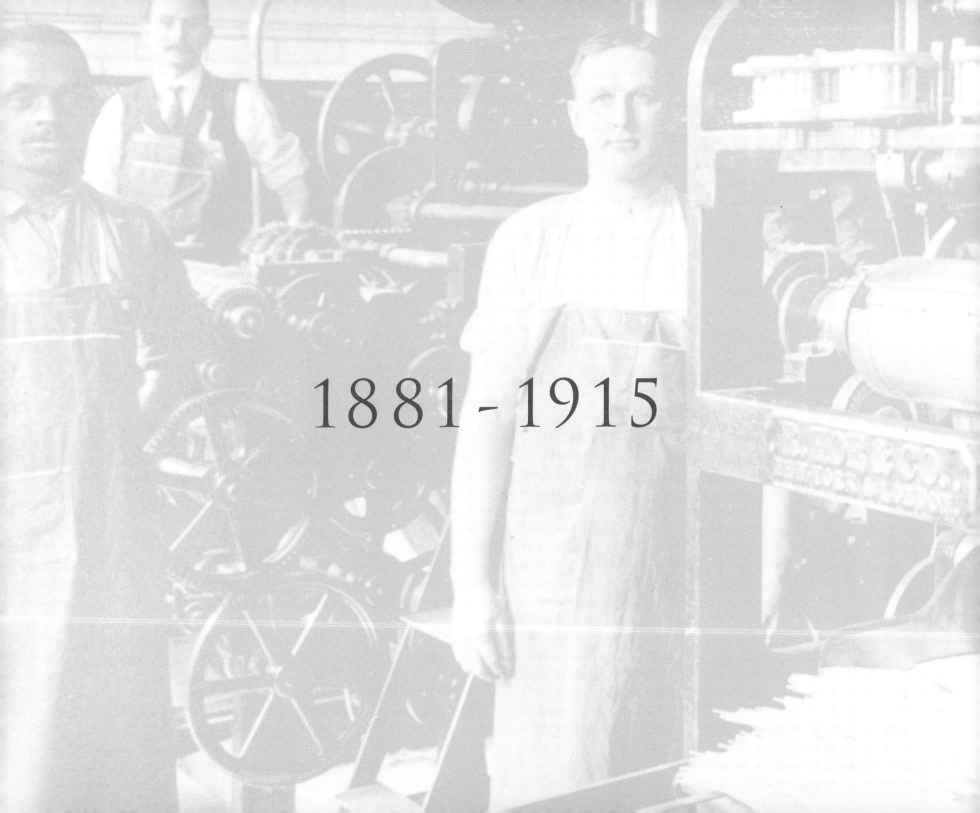

1881 – 1915

CHAPTER 2

INDUSTRIALIZATION AND THE GILDED AGE

As America entered the Gilded Age, the Nation's population was growing, broadening the already substantial domestic market for goods. Significant technical and scientific developments came rapidly and the Government grew in the aftermath of the Civil War. The period saw the apotheosis of the American industrial revolution and developments in printing technology were at the forefront. Faster and better printing presses and the introduction of inexpensive wood pulp-based paper made books, magazines, and newspapers a truly mass media. The introduction of machine typesetting completed the mechanization of printing. At the beginning of this period, print shops were still fundamentally like the craft-based shops stretching back to Gutenberg. By the time it was over, printing took on an industrial face.

Advances in printing technology did not go unnoticed by GPO. The agency's requirements for equipment to meet the rising demand for printed documents were to contribute to an always-evolving state of the art in the industry. In 1878, Public Printer Defrees observed, "Improvements in machinery for the more practical and economical manufacture of newspapers and books are constantly being made and those who do not use them work to great disadvantage." As a result, GPO transformed itself from a large but primarily craft-based operation to a giant factory-city by 1905.

The first signs of this transformation were visible in the steam-powered Adams presses and cylinders presses that were part of the print shop purchased by the Government in 1860. Adams presses, first widely manufactured by R. Hoe & Co. in the 1850s, were a bed-and-platen press, operated by two workers, capable of turning out high-quality work such as book printing at a rate of 500–1000 impressions an hour. Cylinder presses, which were just coming into wide use in the 1860s, were better suited to less-demanding (at least in terms of quality) newspaper and magazine printing.

An Adams press, made by R. Hoe & Co., of the type already in service in Wendell's shop when it became GPO in 1861. This view is at Harper Brothers in New York, but is representative; GPO's rolls listed women in the press division who probably worked as press feeders.

Left: *By 1880, the original Wendell building had been subsumed by many additions and extensions. The building entrance now faced North Capitol Street, in the same position as the present-day main entrance. This engraving probably depicts a much tidier scene than the reality.*

In 1866, Superintendent Wendell had brought in the first perfecting press, a Bullock, fed from a continuous reel or spool of paper. The press printed from stereotype plates (impressions cast from hand-set type) and printed on both sides of the paper. Paper was fed from the reel, cut into sheets by the mechanism, and then carried through the press by tapes and mechanical fingers. The press could deliver 10,000 double-sided sheets in an hour, ten times more than a well-maintained Adams press. With the Bullock press, GPO's industrial transformation began in earnest.

Congress's decision in 1873 to print the newly-named *Congressional Record* at GPO provided further impetus for GPO's industrialization. New, technologically sophisticated presses, as well as supporting machines from electrical generators to binding machinery, were added to the Office's inventory in the name

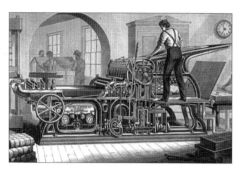

A Cottrell and Babcock two-revolution cylinder press of the type purchased to print the Congressional Record.

of—and with costs accruing against the appropriation for—the *Record*. Public Printer Defrees took such a step in 1878 by contracting for the manufacture by Cottrell & Babcock of specially-designed two-revolution cylinder presses, specifically for the production of the *Record*. When they were delivered, Defrees reported to Congress that "more work can be done on these presses than can be done on 12 Adams presses and by the employment of one third the number of employees…" As printing capacity grew at GPO, so too did the demand for its products, and the number of compositors, pressmen, binders, and other workers steadily increased.

Not only presses were changing. In 1882, the Public Printer's annual report noted the purchase of an "electrical plant, consisting of two dynamos, lamps, and all other necessary fixtures and labor," and soon the motive power for presses and other machinery became electricity. Plates were struck from type using newer and more efficient methods, extending and increasing the efficiency of press runs. Presses continued to grow faster and more efficient. Binding was increasingly mechanized. The stage was set for GPO's years of greatest growth. The last great roadblock to increased productivity remained technologically immovable until the 1880s: Type

continued to be set by hand until the invention of two methods of machine typesetting that, when finally introduced to GPO in 1904, would allow GPO to take its place as "the world's largest printer," a distinction it retained for nearly 80 more years.

Public Printer Rounds

President Chester A. Arthur appointed Sterling Parker Rounds as Public Printer in April 1882. Rounds was born in Vermont in 1828. At the time of his appointment, the Nation was still reacting to the previous year's assassination of President James Garfield by a disappointed office seeker, an event that gave impetus to civil service reform legislation. In January 1883, the Pendleton Act provided for a bipartisan commission to draw up and administer competitive examinations for Federal jobs. Although directed initially to a small percentage of the workforce across the Federal Government, Rounds embraced the concept and implemented it at GPO. He said, "The custom was for each foreman to appoint or

Sterling Parker Rounds (1828-1887), who began to institute the competitive service at GPO.

discharge at will; there was no record aside from the pay-roll, and it was simply impossible for the head of the office to know who was in his employ. …I adopted the rule that the Public Printer…should make all the appointments." A daily record of employees by state was introduced, along with a weekly report showing "appointments, resignations, deaths, transfers, etc."

Rounds was an energetic innovator. The problem of a mob scene one payday per month was solved by dividing the payroll into three sections and paying on the third, eighth, and thirteenth workdays of the month. He renewed old wooden floors and installed new toilets. He abolished the older practice of wetting calendared paper in favor of the more popular method of working dry paper that kept its gloss and finish. He recommended and obtained from Congress 15 days paid annual leave for employees; there previously had been none. He also introduced modern, systematic accounting practices.

Public Printer Benedict

Thomas E. Benedict succeeded Rounds in September 1886, the appointee of President Grover Cleveland. He was appointed again in 1894 in President Cleveland's second term. During his first term, with a workforce of about 2,200, Benedict recommended 30 days paid annual leave, which was granted in 1888. He began the practice of requiring annual reports from division chiefs. He promoted the use of electrotype and stereotype in place of printing directly from type, extending the life of type and making longer press runs more practical. He noted that craft workers, who at that time were paid according to wages set by Congress, were petitioning for better wages, and he went on record saying, "rates of wages as fixed by law are now insufficient." He supported premium pay for night work, acknowledging that it was common practice elsewhere in the trade. In 1888, Benedict cooperated with the JCP in an investigation into allegations of irregularities in making appointments and dismissals from the office. The resulting report exonerated GPO, noting, "the management of the GPO is thoroughly honest and efficient. …It is today turning out more work and better work than has ever been done before in its history…and compares favorably with the best of private printing offices."

On returning for a second term in 1894, Benedict found a workforce of about 3,600, which he set about reducing. The reduction of 700 jobs prompted workers to petition for an extension of civil service protections. The President placed GPO in the classified service in August of that year, and GPO rules for the competitive service were published soon after. Although Benedict remained skeptical of the impact, he acknowledged in 1896 that new employees selected from certified lists worked as well as those previously appointed.

The Printing Act of 1895

The most significant event to occur during Public Printer Benedict's tenure was the passage of the Printing Act of 1895. The Act brought under GPO's control other Federal printing plants then in existence, provided for the production of virtually all other Federal printing at GPO itself, and transferred the position and functions of the Superintendent of Documents to GPO. The Act also provided rules for sizes of editions, established rates of compensation for printers and binders, authorized a system of apprentice training, set up a system of standards and rules for

the selection and purchase of paper and other supplies, defined the basis on which charges for work and prices for documents are set, and outlined the working organization of the Office. In their broad outline, these and other changes formed the basis for the public printing and documents statutes in Title 44 of the U.S. Code that continue to this day.

The most important change brought about by the Printing Act was the transfer of the Superintendent of Documents to GPO, a reform that capped years of efforts by Congress to devise an efficient and effective system for ensuring public access to Government publications. In the early years of the Republic, special acts were passed periodically to distribute particular documents, at that time comprising primarily congressional publications, to State legislatures, governors, colleges and universities in each State, and historical societies. In 1813, the 13th Congress enacted a resolution providing for the distribution of documents on a regular basis to such institutions for that Congress and "every future Congress." This was the statutory antecedent to what was to become the Federal Depository Library Program. Over the next four decades, this system of distribution was carried out variously by the Librarian of Congress, the Clerk of the House of Representatives, and the Secretary of State.

Thomas E. Benedict (1839–1904). He began the practice of paid annual leave and premium pay for night work.

In 1857, the responsibility was transferred to the Secretary of the Interior, and laws were then enacted in 1858 and 1859 transferring the authority to designate the institutions receiving Government documents to Representatives, Delegates, and Senators. Subsequent laws required the Secretary of the Interior to receive, arrange, and distribute documents, to keep accurate statistics on the receipt and distribution of all documents, and to distribute maps and charts as well as books. In 1869, the post of Superintendent of Public Documents was established within the Interior

The Public Documents Library in the early years of the 20th century, after the Public Documents Division moved from leased space into the seven-story annex at the rear of the North Capitol and H Street site. The two-tier iron and steel book stacks were the latest in library design.

Department, and distribution responsibilities were broadened to include executive agency documents.

In spite of these efforts, however, by the 1890s the management of Government documents had become a "hopelessly haphazard operation:"

> Copies of documents were ordered with little regard for public or official interest. Of the 420 official depositories [by 1895], some were overwhelmed by mountains of government publications, while others received no regular distribution at all. Copies ordered for congressional use accumulated in Members' offices until no storage space remained, at which time Senators and Representatives dispatched them to home libraries to crowd shelves often already jammed with other documents that had been obtained by direct distribution. … In addition, no standard system for titling government documents existed. Consequently, practical cataloging was virtually impossible.[17]

By relocating the Superintendent of Documents to GPO, the 1895 Printing Act made it responsible for cataloging and indexing Government publications, distributing documents to depository libraries nationwide, and offering documents for sale to the public; "in fine," according to the *New York Daily Tribune* in December 1894, commenting on the legislation then under consideration, "to render accessible to librarians and the public generally the vast store of Government publications:"

> Under [GPO's] operation the cost of public printing and binding will be materially reduced and a system established which will result not only in a more intelligent distribution of Government publications, but in placing copies of all of them in depositories throughout the country where they will be convenient of access to persons who may desire to consult them. The bill also provides for the distribution among public libraries and other depositories of the vast accumulation of old documents—numbering nearly 1 million volumes—which now occupy valuable space in the Capitol and elsewhere in Washington, and against further accumulations of the same sort.

The Act was signed into law in January 1895. To carry out GPO's new duties, Public Printer Benedict appointed Francis Asbury Crandall the first Superintendent of Documents in March. Crandall immediately began building a staff and organization to carry out the provisions of the act, among them GPO's first librarians, Adelaide Hasse, Edith Clarke, William Burns, and congressional bibliographer J. H. Hickox.

In consolidating the three public access responsibilities under the Superintendent of Documents—sales, library distribution, and cataloging and indexing—the Printing Act created the need at GPO for a comprehensive system of records, a "key" as Superintendent Crandall put it. The turn of the 20th century was a pivotal time in American librarianship, and Crandall, well aware of that world, placed GPO in the middle of the development of library thought and practice by establishing the Public Documents Library. The collection was based on the "vast accumulation of old documents" that seemed to be lodged in every attic and cellar of every Government building, and was to be built up with the addition of all future documents printed at GPO.

The first Superintendent of Documents, Francis Asbury Crandall (1837–1915), a Buffalo newspaperman who remained employed by GPO for many years after his term of office.

The Library was to serve GPO in various ways. It provided the necessary "key" or stock list for both library distribution and sales. It made accurate and consistent cataloging and indexing possible by providing catalogers a basis for research and comparison. All the functions of the Superintendent of Documents grew around the library. The classification system devised by Adelaide Hasse and brought into use by the other GPO librarians including William Leander Post (who was later Superintendent of Documents) was meant to organize and control the library collection. The cataloging information that appeared in the *Monthly Catalog of U.S. Government Publications* was gathered from the items on the library shelves. Eventually it gave the Superintendent of Documents the resources to efficiently answer the many reference queries that came to the Office from libraries and individuals in addition to requests for the purchase of documents.

Adelaide R. Hasse

Women have always worked for the Government Printing Office but until the 20th century few left an individual mark on its history. One exception was Adelaide R. Hasse, the first Superintendent of Documents librarian. In her brief two year career at GPO, she almost single-handedly set up GPO's Public Documents Library and devised the classification system still in use today.

Hasse began her 60-year career in librarianship at the age of 21, when she was employed at the Los Angeles Public Library. She organized the library's documents collection, devised a classification system for them, and began compiling a checklist which became the first of her almost three dozen publications in the field.

In 1895, when Congress established the office of Superintendent of Documents within the Government Printing Office, the Superintendent was made responsible for the sale and depository library distribution of Government publications. Francis A. Crandall was appointed to this new position. When he assumed his post, he confronted a colossal task of sorting and organization. Thousands of documents dating back many years had accumulated helter-skelter in various areas of GPO. More publications clogged the storerooms of the House and Senate. None of these collections was arranged in a systematic way. Crandall quickly realized that a GPO documents library could serve as a "stock key" to the mass of materials in his charge and furnish the reference tools needed to field inquiries.

With these problems in mind, Crandall turned to Adelaide Hasse. In May 1895, she left Los Angeles for Washington, DC to become GPO's first librarian. Her duties included caring for the documents as well as pulling together the many scattered collections stored around the Capitol. Within six weeks of her arrival, nearly 300,000 documents, including duplicates, had been organized and classified. It was at this time that Hasse developed the classification scheme that forms the basis of the one still in use at GPO today.

By 1897, GPO's Public Documents Library had grown from nothing to a well-organized collection of 16,841 printed documents and 2,597 maps. Shortly thereafter, Hasse received and accepted an offer to join the staff of the New York Public Library and build up its documents collection.

By the time of her death in 1953, Adelaide Hasse had become one of the most notable members of her profession. She left behind her a rich legacy of achievement affecting all areas of librarianship, including that of Federal Government documents. Although her GPO years were few, her impact on the agency's role in keeping America informed was great and long lasting.

Gathering the documents began almost immediately on Adleaide Hasse's arrival in Washington, and the library was set up in leased space in the Union Building on H Street a few blocks from GPO. The Public Documents Division (of which the library was part) moved to the H Street annex building sometime after 1900, and the Library was eventually located on the seventh floor of Building 2. It remained central to the life of the Public Documents Division and its public programs until the 1970s, when a critical shortage of space in the main GPO complex forced the Superintendent of Documents functions into leased space in northern Virginia, and the Library collection was judged to be too costly to move and maintain. Most of it was transferred to the National Archives, where it was absorbed into a larger record group. Its only remaining fragment, a portion of the catalog used to control the assignment of Superintendent of Documents Classification numbers, remained in use and in 2009 began to be converted to electronic form to be better incorporated into GPO's overall landscape of catalogs and indexes.

With the centralization of Federal printing and its institutional connection to the Superintendent of Documents, Congress completed development of the "means of acquiring" Government information that Madison had envisioned nearly 70 years earlier. The creation of a system that provided for the selection of documents for public distribution from the comprehensive body of documents printed by the Government marked, in the words of one observer, "the institutional realization of a panoply of reforms pertaining to public printing policy."[18] Through the years, subsequent Public Printers would use the Act to improve on the economic, efficient, and equitable purchase of printing and binding materials as well as the production and distribution of Government documents.

Public Printer Palmer

As GPO's workload grew steadily, the buildings acquired in 1861 underwent multiple additions and modifications. By the end of the 19th century, most of the halfsquare bounded by H Street NW, North Capitol Street, Jackson Alley, and First Street NW (a small part of which held the original Wendell buildings) was occupied by a crazy quilt of interconnected buildings, annexes, sheds, and stables. The latest and among the largest of these was a seven-story tall but extraordinarily narrow annex building built across the western boundary of the property from H Street

GPO about 1900. The Wendell building is still discernible along the H Street side (right).

The seven-story annex, tallest and last of the additions to the original North Capitol and H Street site, completed in 1896.

to Jackson Alley in 1896, in part to house the new Superintendent of Documents functions. The age and inadequacies of this space, however, compelled successive Public Printers to implore Congress with increasing urgency for more, safer, and more efficient space.

Not until the appointment of Frank W. Palmer by President Benjamin Harrison in May 1889, and his subsequent appointment by President William McKinley in March 1897, were these pleas finally heard. A former Representative, Palmer succeeded in convincing Congress of the need for a new building, driven in part by reaction to the deaths of 22 people in 1893 from the structural collapse of Ford's Theatre, used at that time to store War Department records. In July 1898,

Building 1 under construction, probably 1902.

Building 1 soon after its completion in 1903. The most prominent image of GPO from Capitol Hill.

Background image: *Architect's drawing of the façade of the building approved by Congress in 1898–99, now known as Building 1.*

Scale 1/16 inch = 1 foot

U.S. ENGINEER OFFICE
CAPITOL ST. WASHINGTON D.C.
LY SUBMITTED, WITH LETTER OF THIS DATE,
CHIEF OF ENGINEERS U.S. ARMY.

26

John Stephen Sewell
1ST LIEUT. CORPS OF ENGINEERS U.S.ARMY.
CONSTRUCTING ENGINEER.

APPROVED

BRIG. GEN.

PUBLIC

DESIGNED BY

NEW BUILDING FOR GOVERNMENT PRINTING OFFICE

Congress appropriated $225,000 for the purchase by condemnation proceedings of the properties stretching southward to G Street NW, and later that year $2 million was authorized for the construction of a new fireproof building. The foundation was begun in 1899 and the construction was completed in 1903 at a cost of $2,429,000. James G. Hill, a prominent Washington, DC, architect, was chosen to design the building. The preparation of plans and supervision of construction was assigned to Captain John S. Sewell, U.S. Army Corps of Engineers.

Shortly before the building opened, William E. Curtis described it in the Chicago *Record Herald* of May 24, 1903:

> The new printing office will have a floor space of 619,700 square feet, which is equivalent to about fourteen acres or four ordinary city blocks, which is divided into seven floors almost without partitions. Printers need a good deal of light, and it is provided for them by 1,500 windows. One-third of all the wall space is glass, and, in order that this light may not be lost, the walls of the rooms are lined with white enameled bricks which can be washed like a bath tub. …The building is absolutely fireproof, or as near fireproof as any building can be. It is also as substantial as possible, and its walls are built like those of the fortress because type is heavy and printing presses cause considerable vibration, and it would be unfortunate to have the roof and walls cave in and bury 3,597 American citizens under material and machinery that is intended only for the dissemination of intelligence.

> …The outside walls are three feet thick and to construct them 10,000,000 bricks were required. Enclosed within them is a steel framework weighing almost 12,000,000 pounds, which is heavier, perhaps, than the frame of any other building in the country. …The columns, beams, girders, channels, and plates were not made of ordinary stock steel, but were forged to order, and the steel work is so protected that in case of heat being generated by the burning of any material that might be placed in the building, its strength will not be affected by warping.

Now known as Building 1, this structure still stands today on the corner of North Capitol and G Streets, NW, the most prominent image of GPO when viewed from Capitol Hill.

Typesetting Transformed

By the time GPO's new building opened, commercial book and newspaper plants had embraced the introduction of machine typesetting. Two types of machines were in wide use: the Monotype, invented by Tolbert Lanston and manufactured by the Lanston Monotype Company in Philadelphia, and the Linotype, devised by Ottmar Mergenthaler and produced by the Mergenthaler Linotype Company in Baltimore. Both machines were introduced in 1887.

Each was suited to a particular class of work. Monotype was a two-step system. A keyboard produced a punched paper tape, not unlike a player piano roll. When run through a casting machine, the tape produced properly spaced pieces of type from molten lead, which were put directly

The first battery of Monotype keyboards, 1905: The "weird machines that set type by punching holes in paper." This modest group rapidly grew.

An early shot of the Linotype battery, probably ten years after their introduction in 1904.

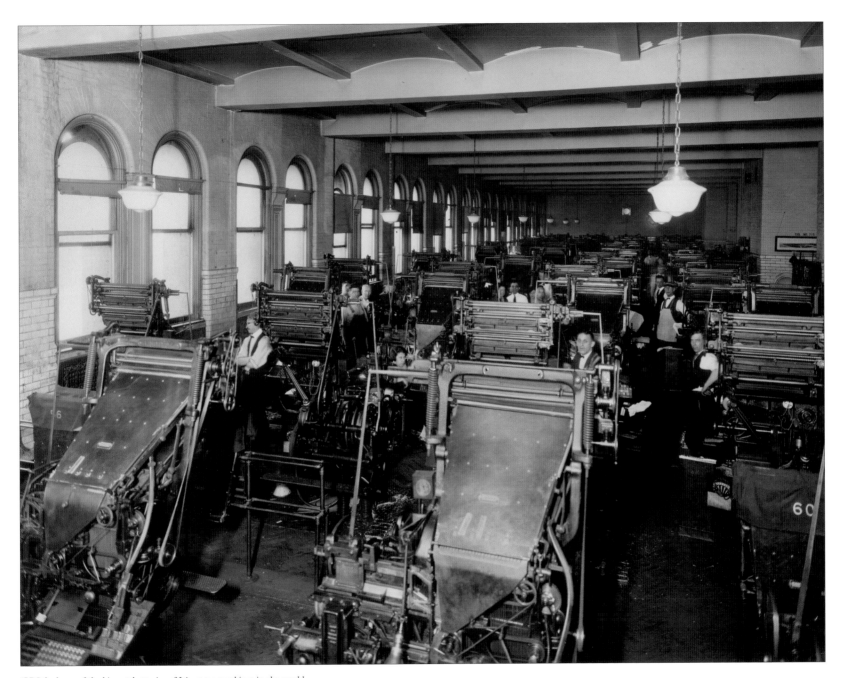

GPO had one of the biggest batteries of Linotype machines in the world.

Monotype casting machines, part of the revolution that changed the typesetting formula from minutes per line to lines per minute.

Making up and imposing Monotype, about 1930.

The Monotype keyboard section in 1915. "The biggest battery of composing machines in the world," according to the Monotype Co.

into forms. These forms could be locked up for use directly on the press, although usually plates were cast. Monotype had as one of its virtues the ability to set up complicated tables and charts. A contemporary advertisement for Monotype proclaimed, "Some of the tables that the Monotype pumps out without effort would puzzle the most skilled hand compositor."[19] The huge Linotype machine, by contrast, cast a full line of type at a time, also from molten lead. Originally built for the newspaper trade, the machines were without parallel for so-called straight work, or text set in columnar blocks on a page.

GPO's new building was designed for a workforce that included about 800 hand compositors. Public Printer Palmer approached the introduction of machine typesetting cautiously, concerned for its ability to produce the required work as well as the potential impact on the workforce. When pressed by Congress in March 1904, he questioned the "economy or adaptability" of machine typesetting, but he ultimately assured the Appropriations Committees of his willingness to experiment, and in June 1904, the *New York Tribune* reported that Palmer had announced the acquisition of a trial group of machines. The *Tribune* commented that "It is also believed that the typesetting machines will not only promote efficiency and decrease cost, but that they will unquestion-

ably be capable of producing the high standard of work required by the Government, and at the same time be of no material injury to the personnel of the establishment."

The initial order was for 46 Linotypes and 28 Monotypes. The machines were quickly embraced and their respective batteries grew rapidly. Linotype entered GPO originally for the production of the *Congressional Record* but was eventually used for a wide variety of other work, including patents. By 1915, GPO used 100 Monotype keyboards and 76 Linotypes, and by 1916, two-thirds of all type set in GPO was Monotype. By 1925, 120 Monotype keyboards, with a comparable number of casters, and 147 Linotypes were in use. GPO boasted the largest number of both machines in the world.

The embrace of machine typesetting completed GPO's industrialization. Over the first 45 years of its existence, presses and bindery machinery had grown steadily faster and capable of larger workloads. The final major process to join the transformation was typesetting, where the new machines changed the measurement of productivity from minutes per line to lines per minute. A skillful hand compositor could be expected to set a line in two minutes; a comparably skilled Linotype operator was capable of four to seven lines per minute. Public Printer Palmer's concerns over machine typesetting proved to be unfounded. Instead, the impact on GPO was striking and almost immediate. By 1915 the Linotype section alone employed nearly as many as the total number of hand compositors at the time the new building opened, and GPO's fully industrialized capacity enabled it to meet the steadily increasing demand for work as the Government grew.

President Roosevelt and His Public Printers

The introduction of machine typesetting and GPO's subsequent growth drew increased public scrutiny as the agency struggled to transform into a fully industrialized concern. The prominence of GPO in the news also drew the close attention of President Theodore Roosevelt, whose involvement with GPO would cost two Public Printers their jobs.

In 1903, President Roosevelt became involved in the case of one William A. Miller. Miller had been hired as an assistant foreman in GPO's bindery, in charge of the blank book section, where he began making reforms in the operation of the section. He denounced the International Brotherhood of Bookbinders and Public Printer Palmer, claiming that

JEFFERSON'S BIBLE

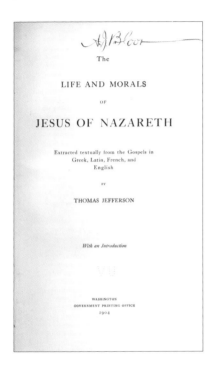

The

LIFE AND MORALS

OF

JESUS OF NAZARETH

Extracted textually from the Gospels in
Greek, Latin, French, and
English

BY

THOMAS JEFFERSON

With an Introduction

WASHINGTON
GOVERNMENT PRINTING OFFICE
1904

Included in GPO's growing workload was an unusual order for a publication that has remained a curiosity to this day: the production of Thomas Jefferson's *Life and Morals of Jesus of Nazareth*, a book that later was to become known as Jefferson's Bible. Prepared between 1794 and 1819, apparently for his own use, the book was a cut-and-paste compendium of selections from the New Testament that Jefferson believed represented "the most sublime and benevolent code of morals which has ever been offered to man," as he later wrote to John Adams. Left out of this collection were all references to miracles and all theological doctrine. It was never published during his lifetime.

Sometime after his death, Jefferson's work made its way to the Smithsonian, where it was discovered years later by Iowa Representative John Lacey. In 1903, Lacey introduced a resolution providing for its printing as a House document. He apparently later had second thoughts about having the Government print the book and, having found a commercial printer to do the work, tried to have the resolution rescinded. But by that time GPO had completed the job, producing 9,642 copies "by the photolithographic process," as the resolution required, at a total cost of $21,258.60. Congress suddenly found itself with 9,000 extra copies of Jefferson's Bible, 3,000 for the Senate and 6,000 for the House. Rather than destroy them, a new congressional tradition was started whereby every new member of Congress was given a copy, continuing until the supply was exhausted in 1957. Jefferson's other contribution to congressional printing—the *Manual of Parliamentary Practice for the Use of the Senate of the United States*—remained in publication by GPO through 1977, and was incorporated into the rules of the House, entitled *Constitution, Jefferson's Manual, and Rules of the House of Representatives*, which is still printed by GPO.

---

they colluded to create a "closed shop," where only union members could be appointed or promoted. Miller was expelled from the union and later dismissed from his position. He took his grievance to the Attorney General, Philander C. Knox, who brought it to the attention of the President and Secretary of Commerce and Labor George Cortelyou. He also filed a formal complaint with the Civil Service Commission, charging that his firing was a violation of their regulations.

The Commission found in Miller's favor and ordered his reinstatement, which Palmer was slow to act on. Meanwhile, President Roosevelt and Secretary Cortelyou's separate inquiry into the matter concluded that the Public Printer had acted improperly. In July 1903, the President directed that Miller be reinstated and that an "immediate and thorough investigation" be conducted. The committee formed for that purpose was critical of Palmer's management of GPO, and their findings were communicated to the Joint Committee on Printing. President Roosevelt directed Palmer to conduct an audit of all accounts, a complete inventory of all materials, obtain bonds for all employees with fiduciary responsibility, and specified that all employees be required to "take the ordinary oath of office," admonishing Palmer, "It seems to reflect most seriously on any Government officer that it should be necessary to make recommendations of this kind for the administration of his office." The incident represented a serious loss of trust between the President and the Public Printer.

Soon after Palmer directed GPO's initial contract for Monotypes and Linotypes in 1904, a second contract for additional Monotypes was signed. The Mergenthaler Linotype Company accused GPO officials of malfeasance in the trial of the machines and the subsequent order of machines from its competitor, Lanston Monotype. The complaint was made at the highest level, leading President Roosevelt to direct the newly-formed presidential Committee on Department Methods (known as the Keep Committee after its chairman, Charles H. Keep) to investigate. The Committee found that the contracts were proper and valid but that Palmer's actions, particularly with regard to two of his foremen, who had given unfavorable testimony against him before the committee, were improper. After the close of the investigation, Palmer brought charges of insubordination against Oscar J. Ricketts and L. C. Hay, and ordered them to meet with him. When news of this retaliation reached the President, he asked for Palmer's resignation and issued an order prohibiting him from meeting with the employees. When the President was informed that the Public Printer had ordered Ricketts and Hay to appear, he immediately removed Palmer from office and named Ricketts Acting Public Printer.

Public Printer Stillings

On hearing the news in 1905 that Public Printer Palmer had been removed, a friend remarked to Charles A. Stillings, "That's a position you ought to have." Stillings, a printer and a member of the New York Board of Trade, agreed and made an appointment to meet President Roosevelt at Oyster Bay, NY. The President was determined to keep politics from guiding his Public Printer appointment, and he was impressed by Stillings' managerial experience and knowledge of printing. While awaiting confirmation, headlines appeared in *The New York Sun* of November 16, 1905: "Printing Office Scandal. Effort To Defeat Confirmation of Stillings. Oscar J. Ricketts, Late Acting Public Printer, Leads The Opposition,

"HOW HAPPY I'D BE WITH EITHER WERE T'OTHER DEAR CHARMER AWAY."

Public Printer Stillings was depicted in political cartoons several times during his tenure. Here he is seen in the Washington Star caught between the partisans of the spelling reform controversy, President Roosevelt at right and Congress (possibly in the person of House Appropriations Committee Chair James A. Tawney).

The Basis of Which Is Alleged To Be the 'Open Shop' Proclivities of Mr. Stillings." Nonetheless, Stillings' confirmation took place without incident. But that headline was prophetic: During Stillings' term, Americans were to hear more about GPO than at any previous time in its history. His troubles began in June 1906, at the close of the first session of the 59th Congress. On July 1, the *New York Times* reported:

> The 1st session of the 59th Congress came to an end at 10 p.m. [on June 30th], hours after it should have…incapacity of the GPO was responsible for keeping both branches in session at least 8 hours beyond the time originally set…The President was obliged to waste the best part of a day sitting around the Capitol with his Cabinet to sign bills…

The rush at the close of a congressional session is a predictable and almost unvarying tradition, and GPO's inability to cope with it seemed incredible. The Senate lambasted the Public Printer with charges of incompetency and poor work and ordered an investigation. The final report, however, not only excused Stillings but in fact showered him with praise for the handling of the situation. The *Times* wryly commented, "The Public Printer will rest undisturbed in possession of the bouquet presented to him when everybody was expecting…a big stick." Stillings had little time to savor his bouquet. On August 24, 1906, the Associated Press reported:

> President Roosevelt has endorsed the Carnegie spelling reform movement. He issued orders today to Public Printer Stillings that hereafter all messages from the President and all other documents emanating from the White House shall be printed in accordance with the recommendation of the spelling reform committee headed by Brander Matthews, professor of English in Columbia University. This committee has published a list of 300 words in which the spelling is reformed. This list contains such words as 'thru' and 'tho' as the spelling for 'through' and 'though.'

The spelling reform movement proposed a number of changes that have lasted to this day, such as removing the "u" from the spelling of color, honor, favor, and rumor. It also had a significant body of respected and articulate supporters, including Samuel Clemens—Mark Twain—as well as Andrew Carnegie, who provided financial support for the movement. But as the Associated Press pointed out, some of its proposed changes seemed outlandish. As a result, the press had a field day with the "reform spelling crusade," and editorials and cartoons abounded. The Supreme Court entered the fray and directed that its opinions be printed in the old style. Congress had the last word when Representative Charles B. Landis of Indiana introduced a resolution on December 13, 1906:

> Resolved, That it is the sense of the House that hereafter in the printing of House documents or other publications used by law or ordered by Congress, or either branch thereof, or emanating from any executive department or bureau of the Government, the House printer should observe and adhere to the standard of orthography prescribed in generally accepted dictionaries of the English language.

REFORMED SPELLING OF THE 300 WORDS

abridgment	develop	judgment	raze
accouter	dieresis	kist	recognize
accurst	dike	labor	reconnoiter
acknowledgment	dipt	lacrimal	rigor
addrest	discust	lapt	rime
adz	dispatch	lasht	ript
affixt	distil	leapt	rumor
altho	distrest	legalize	saber
anapest	dolor	license	saltpeter
anemia	domicil	licorice	savior
anesthesia	draft	liter	savor
anesthetic	dram	lodgment	scepter
antipyrin	drest	lookt	septet
antitoxin	dript	lopt	sepulcher
apothem	droopt	luster	sextet
apprize	dropt	mama	silvan
arbor	dulness	maneuver	simitar
archeology	ecumenical	materialize	sipt
ardor	edile	meager	sithe
armor	egis	medieval	skilful
artizan	enamor	meter	skipt
assize	encyclopedia	mist	slipt
ax	endeavor	miter	smolder
bans	envelop	mixt	snapt
bark	Eolian	mold	somber
behavior	eon	molder	specter
blest	epaulet	molding	splendor
blusht	eponym	moldy	stedfast
brazen	era	molt	stept
brazier	esophagus	mullen	stopt
bun	esthetic	naturalize	strest
bur	esthetics	neighbor	stript
caliber	estivate	niter	subpena
caliper	ether	nipt	succor
candor	etiology	ocher	suffixt
carest	exorcize	odor	sulfate
catalog	exprest	offense	sulfur
catechize	fagot	omelet	sumac
center	fantasm	opprest	supprest
chapt	fantasy	orthopedic	surprize
check	fantom	paleography	synonym
checker	favor	paleolithic	tabor
chimera	favorite	paleontology	tapt
civilize	fervor	paleozoic	teazel
clamor	fiber	paraffin	tenor
clangor	fixt	parlor	theater
clapt	flavor	partizan	tho
claspt	fulfil	past	thoro
clipt	fulness	patronize	thorofare
clue	gage	pedagog	thoroly
coeval	gazel	pedobaptist	thru
color	gelatin	phenix	thruout
colter	gild	phenomenon	tipt
commixt	gipsy	pigmy	topt
comprest	gloze	plow	tost
comprize	glycerin	polyp	transgrest
confest	good-by	possest	trapt
controller	gram	practise, v. and n.	tript
coquet	gript	prefixt	tumor
criticize	harbor	prenomen	valor
cropt	harken	prest	vapor
crost	heapt	pretense	vext
crusht	hematin	preterit	vigor
cue	hiccup	pretermit	vizor
curst	hock	primeval	wagon
cutlas	homeopathy	profest	washt
cyclopedia	homonym	program	whipt
dactyl	honor	prolog	whisky
dasht	humor	propt	wilful
decalog	husht	pur	winkt
defense	hypotenuse	quartet	wisht
demagog	idolize	questor	wo
demeanor	imprest	quintet	woful
deposit	instil	rancor	woolen
deprest	jail	rapt	wrapt

The Washington Star published the complete list of 300 words on September 2, 1906. Many of the spellings that seemed radical in 1906 are common in 2011.

Machine sewing in the Bindery, about 1905. Most of GPO's female employees were bindery workers but. . .

... there were also female press feeders. The Press Division about 1905.

The eye of the spelling reform storm at GPO was the proofroom. Opponents of the changes claimed that they would necessitate hiring a complete second force of proofreaders.

The motion passed unanimously. The President let the Public Printer and the Nation know that the old style was reinstated. But almost immediately another storm appeared on the horizon. In May 1907, Stillings authorized a reduction in force and announced the dismissal of 204 employees, half journeyman bookbinders and half women, mostly sewing operators and goldworkers. This action, Stillings said, was necessitated by changes in printing and binding regulations that caused a reduction of work. A special dispatch to the *Rochester Chronicle* of April 30, 1907, described the resulting impact: "Many pathetic scenes followed the receipt of the dreaded yellow envelopes by the women. A number of them could not refrain from shedding tears. ...Several of them had worked in the printing office for years." Stillings further alienated employees by ordering physical examinations for the elderly workers at GPO, including women. This was reflected in a news item on September 31, 1907: "Many of them are widows of Civil War soldiers and they know that they cannot hop, skip, and jump in competition with boys and young men." Stillings also ordered the removal of mirrors from work areas, prompting one employee to explain on April 27, 1907:

> Yes, we had our own mirrors and they were necessary. In the main dressing room of each of the floors where the women work there is one mirror, but what could a hundred or more girls do before one mirror when everybody wants to leave as soon as the Government has had our day's work? Under the old order it took each of us but a moment to see how we looked and we could go out on the street feeling that we were presentable. From half past 4 o'clock until 6 each day is the only time we have in which to do our modest shopping, and it is a race to get to the stores before they close. Mr. Stillings evidently believes we should leave this building all frowsied up and looking disreputable. Well, we'll fool him, anyhow, for he cannot prevent our carrying little pocket mirrors and the shops will have a run on that article.

The unions also weighed in. A headline in *The Boston American* on March 15, 1907, read "Strike Threatened at U.S. Print Shop." The article went on to say:

Mr. Stillings made the papers again in 1907, with his order that all GPO officers (managers) were to refer to their subordinates as "Mr.," "Miss," or "Mrs." rather than by first names. Although apparently well-intentioned, the order met with some scorn as Stillings' popularity declined.

Because they claim Public Printer Stillings is trying to supplant them with apprentices and unskilled men, the small army of stereotypers and electrotypers at the great government print shop are threatening a strike. At a special meeting a delegation was named to wait on Stillings and present their grievances.

On July 22, 1907, the same newspaper reported:

Resolutions denouncing in vigorous terms Stillings' recent order fining proofreaders for overlooking errors were forwarded today to President Roosevelt and laid before the

Department of Justice by Columbia Typographical Union No. 1. On October 17, 1907, the Central Labor Union of the District of Columbia passed resolutions asking President Roosevelt to remove Charles A. Stillings from office.

Public Printer Stillings, who came to GPO with the President's mandate for organizational efficiency as a touchstone, viewed things differently from his critics. He expressed himself on June 24, 1907, before a Washington, DC, gathering of photoengravers and electrotypers. A reporter noted:

Mr. Stillings said an effort was being made to place the [GPO] on a plane with the best printing establishments in the world. He described how he had found a more or less disorganized force of workmen in many lines; how he had made an attempt to place at the head of several departments experts in their several lines; how he had met with some opposition; how he had been misunderstood in some ways, but how at last it was becoming apparent that the [GPO] is not only abreast with the best establishments of its kind in the world, but the idea was beginning to appear that the true aim is to make it the model printing house of the world.

However noble his aspirations, the political realities of making unpopular decisions quickly overshadowed Public Printer Stillings and, amid many allegations and denunciations, he was suspended by President Roosevelt in February 1908 pending yet another Presidential commission investigation. While the commission's report criticized Stillings, concluding that he "had not been a good judge of men," it also found that he "could not be accused of any intentional wrongdoing."[22] Nonetheless, he was not returned to office, and President Roosevelt appointed his next Public Printer on June 9, 1908.

Public Printer Leech

John S. Leech had learned the printing trade in Indiana. When appointed as Public Printer, he was serving as Public Printer of the recently acquired Philippines. One of the first areas he examined at GPO was wages, and he authorized increases for Linotype and Monotype operators as well as printers, bookbinders, proofreaders, and other occupations requiring special skill. During his brief administration, Leech implemented a detailed system of accounting, showing "monthly the total cost of operation, daily the amount of wages earned, and at any moment the amount of purchases, the total expenditures to date, and the outstanding obligations." The system was considered to be of "comparative simplicity" and "logical arrangement." Owing to poor health, Leech resigned on December 1, 1908, the Public Printer of shortest tenure. However, his stay apparently was long enough to restore good relations between the Office of the Public Printer and GPO's employees. On Leech's last day at GPO, more than 1,000 employees met with him to wish him well.

Public Printer Donnelly

President Roosevelt's final appointment as Public Printer, made in the waning days of his term on December 1, 1908, was Samuel B. Donnelly, a former president of the International Typographical Union. He served through the term of Roosevelt's successor, President William Howard Taft, until June 25, 1913. Donnelly was well known to Roosevelt, who had previously appointed him to a number of special commissions. One of Donnelly's early suggestions, made in his annual report for 1909, related to the eighth or attic floor of the new building. He observed:

> The majority of employees of the Government Printing Office partake of the noonday meal in the workrooms in which they are employed. Food is carried into the workrooms in large quantities and distributed from convenient points. This method is unhealthful and insanitary, increases the difficulty of keeping the office clean, and attracts insects destructive to certain classes of material.

He went on to request authority to construct skylights in the roof and to use the area as a lunchroom. This recommendation would wait for nearly 20 years to be instituted.

Donnelly also set about securing new business. He was able to report in December 1910: "In February we undertook the work of printing the postal cards. On this work many difficulties were met with, particularly

John S. Leech served only six months as Public Printer, the shortest tenure on record.

Samuel B. Donnelly had been president of the International Typographical Union and was Theodore Roosevelt's third Public Printer.

owing to paper and mechanical troubles. At the date of the submission of this report, however, the work is up-to-date. The Government Printing Office printed in the month of October 156,834,000 cards." Postal card production remained a mainstay of GPO's business until 2007, when electronic mail and other digital messaging finally led to the end of demand for postal cards. He also reported the JCP had approved his proposal to use a lighter weight paper for the *Congressional Record* and other Government printing, in addition to eliminating other unneeded paper stocks, in order to achieve savings.

Donnelly became involved in an incident in 1911 that reflected both the developing face of the GPO workforce and that of its home in the District of Columbia. During the construction of a garage, the Civil Service Commission certified six bricklayers and one laborer for work on the project. After a few days on the job, the bricklayers let it be known that they wanted the laborer, a black man, removed from the project. When this was not done, they walked out. The Civil Service Commission then certified six new bricklayers, who happened to be black men. Vociferous criticism was leveled at the Public Printer for refusing to dismiss the laborer, and for replacing the bricklayers who had left. Donnelly clearly

Many binding processes became mechanized around the turn of the 20th century. This is probably the Congressional Record *line, 3rd floor, Building 1, between 1905 and 1910.* (Library of Congress)

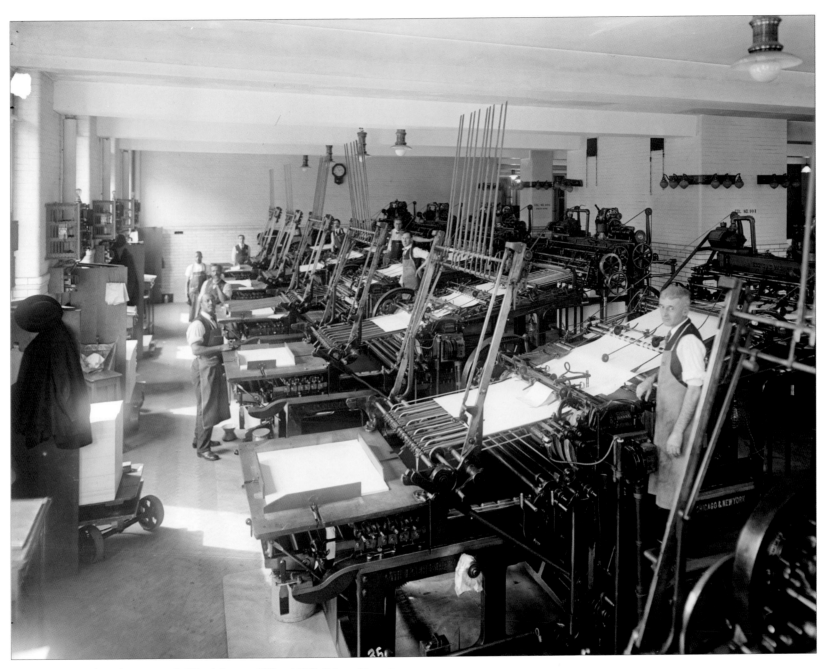

Sheet-fed presses in the main pressroom, Building 1, between 1905 and 1910. (Library of Congress)

GPO's Stables

For more than 50 years, horse-drawn transport was a vital part of GPO's structure. When the Federal Government purchased Cornelius Wendell's print shop for the newly established Government Printing Office in 1861, the price included a stable and carriage house, one black horse, one bobtail bay horse, one wagon, one carryall (a light covered carriage for four or more people), two sets of single harness, two wheelbarrows, one large harness closet, and one large closet.

In 1881, GPO acquired a new stable and wagon house, which could handle 4 to 6 wagons and 8 to 12 horses. In 1896, GPO built a new, 7-story extension that claimed the stable land, and the displaced horses, wagons, and stablemen moved to rented quarters. In 1903, GPO leased a stable and carriage house on L Street. The new structure had a 22-horse capacity and stood two stories high, the second story serving as a hay loft.

The cost of a horse generally ranged from $150 to $200. GPO's largest single transportation expense was for forage, followed by horseshoeing and harness and wagon repair. In a 1942 interview, James F. Fletcher, who came to GPO in 1906 as a carriage driver, said that horses were bought based on bids stating the required quality and breeding. GPO's veterinarian, Cornelius C. Weeks, examined each horse before purchase. Weeks received about $2,000 a year from 1905 to 1912 for his services. Drivers like Fletcher earned an entering wage of 25 cents an hour

In 1910, Public Printer Samuel B. Donnelly ordered a study to determine whether the Office's transportation needs would best

The GPO stable, about 1903, a leased building on L Street. The carriage at left is identified as the Public Printer's because it has a pair of horses. All other GPO wagons and carriages had only one.

The GPO "motor pool" about 1912.

be served by horse-drawn or automotive transport. The study concluded that if autos replaced wagons, GPO's total transportation expense, excluding wages, would be substantial. In 1912, six electric trucks were purchased for $17,373. Charging panels and circuits and a new garage cost another $19,160.25. All but six horses and two wagons were sold as surplus. By this time, Fletcher and his coworkers had been retrained in the new technology, learning to drive by practicing turning and backing in the stable until they were ready for the road. In 1942, Fletcher was still a driver for GPO, an early example of accommodation to changing technology in the workplace.

GPO entered the automobile age in 1912 with the purchase of six Baker electric trucks, built in Cleveland, Ohio.

expressed himself on this matter, and was quoted by *The Reformer* of Richmond, VA, on November 11, 1911:

> I am loyal to union principles when they stand for protection and for fair play to all concerned. Negro bricklayers work side-by-side with white bricklayers in the Washington and other Navy yards. I cannot see why in the case of the work to be done at the Government Printing Office, the white bricklayers should expect an exception to be made in their favor. There are 400 Negro employees in the Government Printing Office… [who] work in the various departments side-by-side with other employees. …I wish to declare with all emphasis that any employee of this department who tries to precipitate the devilish stricture of race prejudice will be immediately dismissed and will not again be employed!

Donnelly proved himself a reformer in other ways. He reported to Congress in 1911:

> There are employed in the Government Printing Office more than 250 persons above the age of 65, and it would be of advantage to the Government to provide for the retirement of those who have given to the public service the best years of their lives and who may be unable to perform an average day's work. This could be equitably accomplished through the adoption of a plan which would in effect amount to an annuity to each employee upon arriving at the age of retirement or upon becoming disabled. …Such a plan would result in saving a large proportion of the amount that it is conceded generally is now lost through the superannuation of employees, and would at the same time be an act of justice to the individual and a recognition of long and faithful service.

The Civil Service Employees' Retirement Act did not take effect until 1920, but Public Printer Donnelly helped sow the seeds. By the end of his term, the full industrialization of GPO had laid the groundwork for major improvements to be made in the worklife of GPO's employees at "the big shop." ❧

"The Brainery" – proofreaders at work in the proofroom, about 1900.

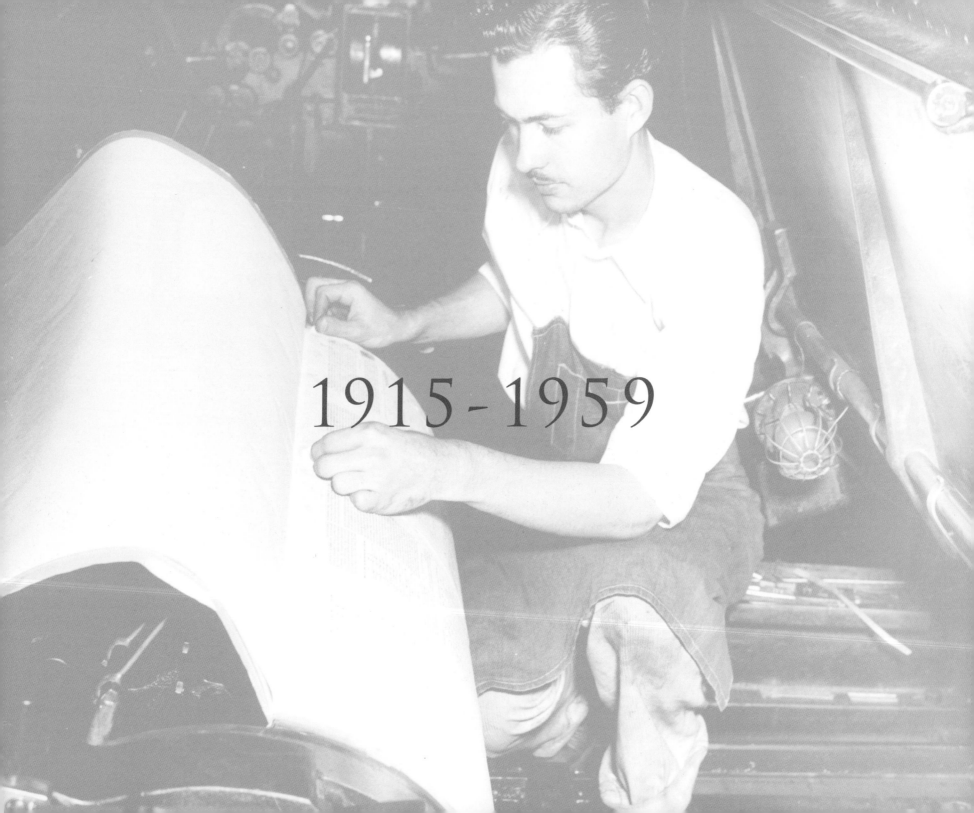

1915-1959

CHAPTER 3

THE PROGRESSIVE ERA, THE DEPRESSION, AND WORLD WAR

By the early 20th century, the character of Government publishing had changed substantially. In the early days of the Republic the bulk was congressional. By the end of the 19th century executive agencies both fueled and fulfilled public demand for a wide variety of information, and it soon became an expectation that the Government would provide everything from reports on scientific endeavor and geographical exploration to crop research and demographic data. In the decades between 1885 and 1905 the number of publications issued by the Government doubled. The industrialization of Government printing enabled GPO to meet this demand as printing production and distribution became increasingly efficient and economical.

Through the last decades of the 19th century and into the 20th, critics and defenders alike commented on the vast growth of Government publishing. Critics tended to focus on the ever-expanding output of agencies. In 1906, William S. Rossiter, one of the leading voices for Government effi-

Left: *"The finest view of Washington and the surrounding country that is to be had." GPO's roof terrace about 1935.*

ciency who later served as Acting Public Printer, wrote in an article titled "What Shall We Do With Public Documents?," "Publications…which are intended, directly or indirectly, for the benefit of the public are quite another matter [from congressional publications]…any one is privileged to inquire how they came into existence, and whether they serve their purpose most effectively." Such criticisms were primarily leveled at agencies rather than at GPO, and as the turmoil of the Theodore Roosevelt administration subsided, newspapers and magazines, both in the printing trade press and for general readers, turned out a stream of articles about the wonders and capacities of "the big shop"

Cornelius Ford, appointed by Woodrow Wilson in 1913, had been president of the New Jersey State Federation of Labor.

on North Capitol Street. These wonders and capacities would be put to the test in the coming decades to fulfill the vastly increased requirements of the Government for the printing needed to meet the emergencies of two World Wars and the Great Depression.

Public Printer Ford and World War I

In June 1913, newly-elected President Woodrow Wilson appointed Cornelius Ford, president of the State Federation of Labor in New Jersey, as Public Printer. Shortly after his appointment, Ford submitted his recommendations for plant modernization to Congress, including upgrading GPO's Monotype and Linotype machines. In 1914, he directed the replacement of obsolete presses and installed an offset press, marking the introduction of this technology to GPO. A year later, he urged the adoption of offset printing, which would "provide for a wider range of work at a greater speed." He also pressed for a new building to relieve overcrowding and provide more space for expanded press operations.

The issue of GPO wages preoccupied Ford throughout his term. At that time, GPO wages were still fixed by Congress. This inflexible system prevented adjustments to keep wages commensurate with commercial wages, making it difficult to attract and retain skilled workers. One of Ford's first recommendations to Congress was to increase the wages of compositors and bookbinders, and he was to repeat this same request in annual reports for 1914–1917. In his final report for 1920, he pointed out with some exasperation:

> For the past two or three years only by promises of his utmost endeavor with Congress for relief has the Public Printer been enabled to retain sufficient efficient employees on the legislative rolls to take care of the ever increasing demands of Congress, the departments, and the general public. Within the past year the office has lost by resignation the services of many of its best paid and most efficient employees, and the good of the service impels this appeal to the Congress for a proper adjustment of these rolls. …Owing to the seriousness of the situation it is urgently recommended that Congress take favorable action so that the salary and wage rate in the Government Printing Office will compare with the salary and wage rate paid in commercial establishments doing similar work.

Ford promoted a number of health and safety measures. His annual report for 1914 mentions: "A 'rest room' has been installed on the fifth floor of the new building for women employees who may become exhausted during working hours. The room is under the supervision of the medical and sanitary officer. I consider it a very humane and necessary adjunct to the office." In 1915 he reported: "Realizing that the health of employees in the Linotype section was being endangered by fumes and noxious gases arising from melted metal in the Linotype pots, I installed

a ventilating system in that section. …The installation of this system has resulted in a very material change for the better in the atmosphere of the room and the general working conditions." He also noted that: "All faucets were removed from drinking fountains throughout the buildings and replaced with bubbling fountains…this replacement was a decided advance in sanitation." Ford believed vacations were an important source of rest and renewal for employees. He expressed satisfaction at a legal opinion on the subject issued by GPO's comptroller: "A decision dated February 15, 1915, definitely decided that employees of this office are entitled to leave of absence with pay for 30 working days each year. The decision was fair and just. …" Like Public Printer Donnelly, Ford also urged a pension for GPO workers.

Ford's greatest challenge was in guiding GPO to meet the enormous demand for printing following the declaration of war in April 1917. Full-scale national mobilization generated mountains of urgent and rush work for preparedness and war activities in addition to the continuing demand for congressional and agency printing. War demand from the Army included "millions of copies of drillbooks, handbooks, regulations, etc., clothbound, for immediate delivery. The Navy also needed vast quantities of printing and binding…." Among the items GPO printed were "75 million thrift cards, 25 million questionnaires and blanks, 27 million notices of classifications, and numerous orders ranging from one to five million each. Agriculture was furnished many millions of posters, pamphlets, circulars…" and other work. Along with this workload was secret and confidential work, performed by GPO "under strict and iron-clad regulations," and the work formerly produced by printing branches located in the State, War, and Navy Buildings, which was transferred to GPO by Congress in March 1917. Included in the wartime printing was the daily production of the *Official U.S. Bulletin*, carrying regulatory and related information from the Committee on Public Information, a precursor of what would later become a mainstay of GPO's production operations, the *Federal Register*. Billings for GPO doubled during Ford's term, from $6.6 million in 1913 to $12.2 million in 1918.

To handle this demand, GPO hired 900 more employees and put most divisions on a 24-hour a day, 7-days a week work schedule, with additional expenses for overtime and night work. A pre-war program to retire obsolete equipment, especially presses, helped GPO meet the

A MILITARY FUNERAL

America entered the First World War in 1917. Thousands of inexperienced but eager young men poured into France, bolstering the weary forces of the Allies in their struggle against Imperial Germany.

By 1921 the Government Printing Office, like the rest of the country, was caught up in its own concerns. Yet deep feelings about the war still remained. In August 1921, those feelings would emerge because of a unique event — a military funeral held in GPO.

Charles Addison Rhett Jacobs was one of three GPO employees killed in action during the First World War. He went to work at GPO in 1914. In 1917 he enlisted in the Marine Corps. He participated in active operations in the Chateau-Thierry sector and the Champagne offensive, rising to the rank of corporal. He was killed in action on October 3, 1918 and buried temporarily in France.

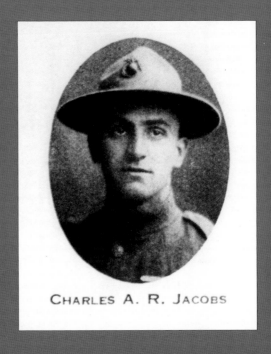

CHARLES A. R. JACOBS

In 1921, Jacobs' mother, Mrs. Roberta Jacobs, approached Public Printer George Carter, saying that "Her son's life was centered in the Government printery before his entry into the service and…no better tribute could be paid his memory than a funeral from the Office in which he and his friends had worked." Carter gave his permission for the service to be held within GPO on Wednesday, August 21, at 12 noon.

The body arrived on Tuesday, August 20. That night, Jacobs lay in state on the first floor landing of Building 1, watched over by a Marine guard. The next day at noon, GPO veterans of all wars were excused from work to allow them to attend the funeral. Representatives of the American Legion, Spanish-American War Veterans, the Grand Army of the Republic, and the Boy Scouts filled the staircase and lobby. Other guests included Secretary of the Navy Edwin Denby, Marine Major General John A. Lejeune and other Navy and Marine officers, and GPO's top officials. The casket was surrounded with an array of floral tributes, including an immense wreath of roses from President and Mrs. Harding.

The funeral procession traversed the Capitol grounds to what is now Constitution Avenue, where it was met by several cars which transported its members and the casket to Arlington National Cemetery. The cortege was composed of a detachment of Marines and a group of GPO veterans, many wearing their old uniforms.

In 1926, the GPO work force purchased and erected two bronze tablets as an honor roll of those who served in the war. Years later, photographs of GPO's World War II dead were placed there. In the 1980s, new tablets commemorating those who served in World War II, the Korean Conflict, and the Vietnam Era, designed and manufactured in-house by GPO employees, were added to what is now officially designated as the GPO Veterans Memorial.

THE PERSHING LINOTYPE

The Model 5 Linotype machine in Chaumont, France, with Corporal Jimmie Kreiter of the 29th Engineers Battalion at the keyboard.

Mergenthaler Model 5 Linotype No. 14168R, otherwise known as the Pershing Linotype, was shipped to Pierre Lafitte & Company, Paris, France, on June 6, 1910. When shipped, it was equipped to cast slugs .918 high, the standard then used in France.

Seven years later, America declared war on Germany and an American Expeditionary Force soon embarked for France. Once there, General John J. Pershing set up his headquarters in the town of Chaumont. One of his most pressing needs was for printing facilities to produce maps, charts, booklets, summaries of information, and orders. Pershing's staff quickly located two Linotype machines in a small French printing plant and transported them by canal and truck to Chaumont. One of these machines was the Pershing.

According to Corporal James M. "Jimmie" Kreiter, a Linotype operator who later worked at GPO, "There were 10 of us—9 printers and 1 pressman. At Chaumont we established ourselves at Camp Babcock, better known as pneumonia hollow." Fourteen-hour days were not unusual. As more men joined the unit, two shifts were set up. Kreiter later described the work routine as "much like our work period here in the Office. Literally the night side had its 'Record' and the day side its 'Federal Register.'"

When the American forces advanced, the Pershing and other machines were installed in trucks as part of a fully-equipped printing unit run by the 29th Engineers. This mobile print shop followed the commanding general for the remainder of the war, occasionally subjected to heavy German shellfire.

The Pershing Linotype came home in 1920. After reconditioning, it was transferred to GPO. In 1926, the International Association of Printing House Craftsmen presented Public Printer George H. Carter with a tablet bearing the following inscription: "IN HONOR OF A LINOTYPE THAT SERVED ITS COUNTRY ON THE BATTLEFIELDS IN FRANCE . . . THERE UPON A THROBBING MOTOR TRUCK MID SHOT AND SHELL THIS MACHINE TYPED GEN. PERSHING'S COMMANDS TO AMERICA'S VICTORIOUS ARMY." In 1940, the Pershing Linotype was transferred to the Apprentice Section for use in training and in 1956 was placed in GPO's Harding Hall as a tribute to its unique record of service to the Nation.

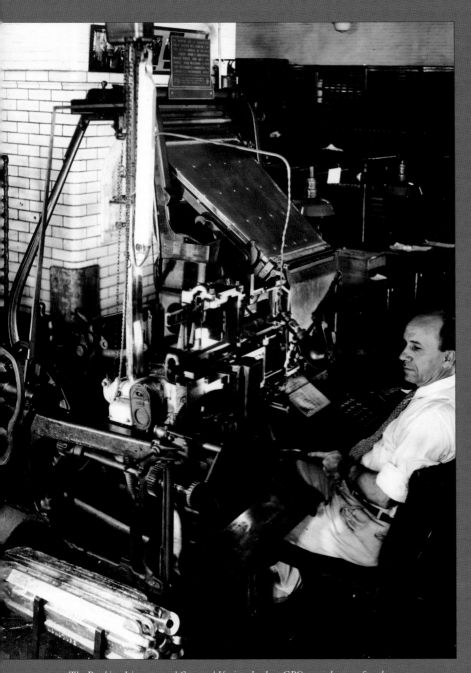

The Pershing Linotype and Corporal Kreiter, back at GPO several years after the war.

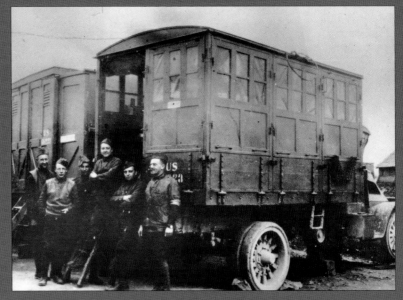

The 29th Engineers with the trucks that formed the mobile printing battalion.

The print shop at Camp Babcock in Chaumont, better known as "Pneumonia Hollow".

crisis, as did the ingenuity of employees in making combinations of press forms, resulting in greater productivity. Wartime increases in the cost of materials and supplies were handled within GPO's scale of prices. Paper was a difficult commodity to obtain during the war, especially after the Joint Committee on Printing refused to award paper contracts at inflated wartime prices, requiring Public Printer Ford to resort to spot buys on the open market and direct personal appeals for the required stocks. To meet a nonstop schedule, plant and equipment maintenance was subordinate to keeping the presses running, and GPO turned increasingly to its own resources, establishing its own ink production capability, making marbled endpapers and carbon papers in-house, and salvaging and re-melting type to save money. During this period, GPO employees suffered approximately 1,600 accidents, an incidence considered low at the time, but more than double the number sustained in 1910.

The greatest sacrifice of the era, however, was made by the 338 GPO employees who served during the war, and the 10 who did not return. In 1926, these were memorialized on the landing above the entrance to GPO Building 1 in plaques paid for by employee contributions. One of these employees, Corporal Charles A. R. Jacobs, had his flag-draped coffin rest on the landing on the evening before his burial in Arlington National Cemetery.

Following World War I, Congress sought to further centralize, or recentralize, Government printing in GPO. Although GPO's originating legislation in 1860 and the Printing Act of 1895 both required all printing for the Government to be performed through GPO, the emergency of World War I prompted Federal agencies to resort to new technologies for disseminating the typewritten word—mimeographing and multigraphing—with a resulting proliferation of Federal publications that escaped the documents system established in GPO. The Printing Act of 1919 sought to restore that system by giving the Joint Committee on Printing approval power over the establishment of printing operations elsewhere than GPO.

Perhaps the real reason for the 1919 act, however, was a provision it contained giving the JCP the power to approve agency publications. Much of the printed matter then being produced by agencies was sympathetic to President Wilson's proposal to create the League of Nations, a proposal that the majority then comprising the JCP vigorously opposed. In 1919

and 1920, the JCP eliminated more than 100 agency periodicals it considered to be unnecessary under its authority to remedy waste and duplication in Government printing. President Wilson apparently believed the publications approval provision in the 1919 Printing Act was temporary. When the 1921 appropriations act for the Government tried to make the provision permanent, he vetoed the bill. His veto message to Congress said the JCP's authority was an "invasion of the province of the President" and would allow the Committee to "determine what information may be given to the people of the country by the executive departments." His veto was sustained, and subsequently the authority over agency publishing decisions was given to the newly created Bureau of the Budget. By then, President Wilson had left office and opposition to the League of Nations no longer was a concern. GPO was caught in the middle of this exchange and since that time it has been careful not to exercise any editorial control over the materials it is given to print.[23]

George H. Carter was Chief Clerk to the Joint Committee on Printing for 12 years before being appointed Public Printer by President Harding.

Public Printer Carter and the "Big Shop"

After the surge of demand for GPO services during World War I, the agency settled into a period of sustained growth and prosperity in the 1920s, led by President Warren G. Harding's appointment of George H. Carter as Public Printer in April 1921. Carter was an attorney from Iowa who had served 12 years as chief clerk, or staff director, of the JCP when he was nominated. President Harding, fondly remembered by GPO as the "printer President" because of his background as a newspaper publisher in Ohio, had deferred in his choice for Public Printer to Senator Reed Smoot of Utah, chairman of the Joint Committee. Smoot described Carter as "capable and courteous" with "eminent good judgment and unflagging industry," a far cry from the notorious "Ohio Gang" of appointees and hangers-on who would dog Harding's time in office and tarnish his legacy. Carter was to serve as Public Printer 12 years, up until that time the longest term ever served in that office.

The renovations created a full eighth story with a cafeteria, auditorium, employee lounge, and bowling alley, as well as a new photoengraving plant and storage.

The first of many incarnations of GPO's duckpin bowling alley, in the 1920s. The bowling alleys remained a GPO fixture until the 1960s.

Among Public Printer Carter's first actions was the reconstruction of the top story of Building 1 to create new space, most of it devoted to "employee rest and recreation."

Employees bowled on dinner breaks and after their shifts, and several teams existed on all shifts. This photo is from the late 1930s

The employee lounge, or "Green Room," provided space for meetings and relaxation. The cases display trophies from teams and organizations that sprang up during Public Printer Carter's term.

GPO's roof terrace about 1935, showing the electric signs that once advertised the agency.

THE EARLY YEARS OF HARDING HALL

When George H. Carter assumed the office of Public Printer on April 5, 1921, he found a budget surplus – an unexpected balance of about $2.4 million. These funds were available for the Public Printer to spend on stock, equipment, and the "betterment of plant." With these funds, Carter literally raised the roof. Building 1, completed in 1903, originally consisted of seven floors and an attic space topped by a pitched roof. Carter decided to raise the sides to the level of the roof's center. Although a new photoengraving facility and storage area were part of Carter's building project, his heart was really in the construction of a cafeteria and recreation rooms for GPO's employees. In-plant facilities would serve to improve morale and health while increasing efficiency and productivity.

When the time came to christen the new assembly hall, Carter honored incumbent President Warren G. Harding, the man who had appointed him Public Printer. Lest critics assume he was merely currying favor with the genial ex-newspaperman from Ohio, Carter adroitly noted that the President's background made him America's first "printer President."

Harding Hall's first informal gathering of employees occurred on Christmas Eve of 1921. Those who participated saw a far different hall than exists today. Although the 68-foot width was the same, it was considerably shorter in length and had smaller seating capacity. The low ceiling seemed to loom directly above the heads of the audience.

Harding Hall in its original form before the further raising of its roof in 1930. The camera is about halfway back; the present hall facing the doors and the elevator lobby beyond.

GPO has marked the holiday season with celebrations for employees and their families that have always included a Christmas tree and a model train layout. This is probably 1922.

Although just a few feet above the floor of the hall, a semicircular row of footlights illuminated a small but serviceable platform for drama or speechmaking. Thanks to employee contributions, a $1,600 grand piano adorned the stage while an upright piano for dancing was available. There was also a mechanical player with violin attachment installed by its manufacturer. During the week, this machine provided dance music for the lunch period.

Those GPO employees who preferred live music for dancing had to wait until Friday, when an all-GPO orchestra played from 11:30 a.m. to 1 p.m. A night unit played from 11 p.m. to 12 midnight. More than 20 employees practiced on their own time and brought their own instruments to these lunchtime concerts.

The end of each year also brought holiday gatherings for children, featuring decorated trees and toy trains — another Office tradition still observed today.

Later in his term, Carter sought and won approval for a further renovation. In 1930, when the new Harding Hall was dedicated, it looked much as it does today. Old Harding Hall was gone — but the memories lingered on.

A GPO basketball team from 1942.

Carter said that the President "…instructed me to operate the 'big shop' on a strictly business basis, to stop waste and extravagances…as far as was within the power of the Public Printer." He was well situated for that work, with his detailed knowledge of GPO and JCP functions and the goodwill of both the oversight committee and appropriators. He was able to begin with his reforms immediately. By June 1921 he cited a substantial list of accomplishments in his first annual report, including an unexpended balance of receipts of $2.4 million, which he directed at workplace repairs and improvements rather than the stockpiling of paper and other supplies that usually happened at the end of a fiscal year.

Carter's first years in office were characterized by three principal themes: employee welfare and workplace improvement, reform and expansion of the business, and modification and reform of the labor-management relationship. Each of these themes played out in a decade of vigorous, expanding business as well as lasting changes to GPO's culture and organizational structure. He took over an office bustling with postwar activity and 4,388 employees on the rolls. The number of employees had actually declined from a wartime high of 5,300, and would continue to drop throughout the decade to 4,072 in 1928.

The workplace improvements ordered by Carter from the surplus of 1921 made a range of progressive reforms and improvements possible. The roof of Building 1, a pitched cement roof behind the square Romanesque façade, had cracked and was causing leaks that threatened expensive machines and supplies on the seventh floor. Carter had plans drawn and quickly won JCP approval to make the roof flat, effectively adding a full eighth story of new space, which was devoted to "a much needed photoengraving plant, a better location for metal and storage rooms, an adequate cafeteria, and suitable rest and recreation rooms for employees." Included in those "rest and recreation rooms" were an auditorium, which was named for the President (perhaps the only tribute to Harding in a Federal building in Washington, DC), a large and comfortably furnished lounge/meeting room, and much-beloved duckpin bowling alleys. A rooftop terrace was installed with "the finest view of Washington and the surrounding country that is to be had anywhere in the city," according to Carter.

In defending these improvements from critics who called them "costly playthings," Carter set forth a classically Progressive Era manifesto for his administration:

> The experience of the most successful manufacturers of today, nearly all of whom have adopted the modern method of helping employees better fit themselves for their daily work, clearly shows that such comforts and conveniences as are now being installed…are not only worthwhile from a humanitarian point of view but are also profitable from a merely commercial aspect, owing to the greatly increased efficiency that results from a well contented and physically fit force of employees.

Sports teams were a popular feature of the GPO scene over many years. This baseball team from the 1920s is from the era when GPO, like all Federal agencies, was racially segregated.

The new cafeteria was employee-managed and served a full menu on all shifts.

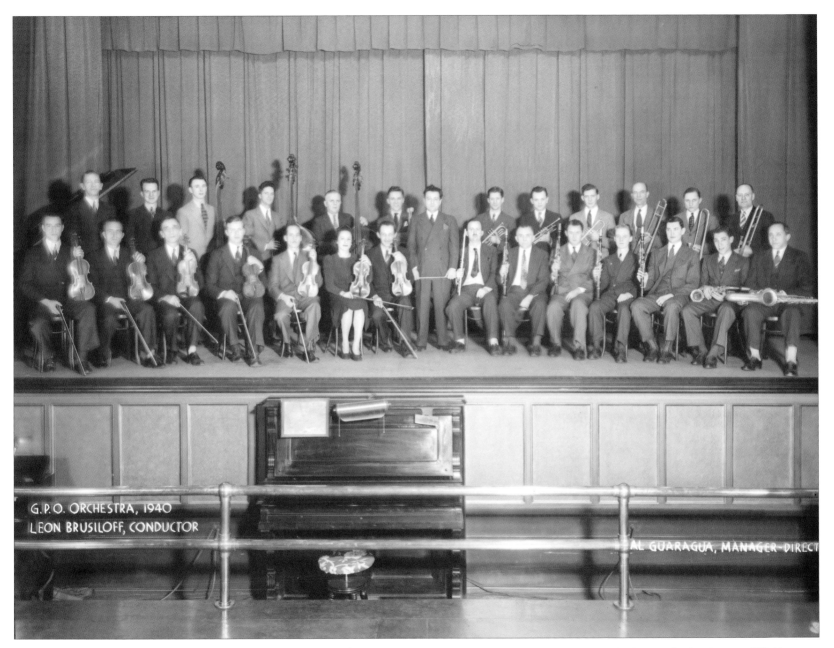

Among the many employee welfare and recreation organizations that became part of the life of GPO, the employee orchestra played during lunch hours, for dances, and at functions around Washington. This shot is from the 1940s.

With these facilities provided, Carter looked to employees to direct and manage activities. An employee association was formed to operate the cafeteria and sponsor employee activities. The GPO Cafeteria and Recreation Association charged dues of one dollar and, in addition to operating the cafeteria, sponsored sports teams, clubs, outings, excursions, and other activities. During this period GPO gained its own chorus and an orchestra that played on Fridays at the dinner breaks on the day and night shifts. The Association began the popular Christmas parties for employees and their families featuring the large Christmas tree and model train layout in Harding Hall. The Cafeteria and Recreation Association existed in some form for nearly 70 years, lasting until the mid-1990s.

For the public, Carter ordered the establishment of a retail bookstore on the first floor of GPO's documents building, then located behind the original Wendell building along H Street. The store was "designed for the convenience of the public who formerly had to ride in a freight eleva-tor to the sixth floor," and was meant to take advantage of the increased amount of local sales of Government documents to the growing number of national organizations locating their headquarters offices in Washington, DC. The store was later relocated to GPO Building 1, where it continues to operate today.

In obeying the command to operate GPO on a "strictly business basis," Carter requested that the method for payment of agency work be revised by Congress. Since the Printing Act of 1895, funds appropriated for printing by executive agencies were paid directly to GPO. This system placed an administrative burden on GPO to account for the funds, limited the agencies' control over their own expenditures, and left little incentive to curtail waste. Carter's proposal, adopted in 1922, directed that all agency appropriations for printing be put in a single fund in each agency specifically for printing. In order to have funds at the beginning of each year, GPO was appropriated a "working capital" fund, which was repaid to the

Analyzing paper in the Testing Section, another of Carter's innovations.

The Testing Section manufactured inks and adhesives for every purpose in the plant.

Treasury as new work was billed and paid. This fund, later modified in 1954, continues today as GPO's revolving fund.

Carter reorganized much of the Office, both in the printing plant and the Superintendent of Documents operation. He began a department with a laboratory devoted to testing and monitoring the quality of printing materials like paper and type metal, achieving substantial savings immediately. A dedicated department for job planning was created that greatly improved service to agencies by making the writing of job specifications more consistent and standardized, thereby improving the plant's ability to deliver economical and better quality work. Although the number of employees declined during much of Carter's term, the volume and value of work steadily grew. By 1924, more type was being set and more sheets were coming off the presses than at any other time, including the height of World War I. GPO's capacity and plant became known everywhere as "the world's largest."

Building 1, which was ample at its opening in 1903, was already cramped by the time Carter took office. In 1926 Congress authorized $1,250,000 for an eight-story addition and garage to be built to the west of that building, along G Street NW. The addition, now known as Building 2, closely matches the style of the 1903 building on the exterior and is virtually indistinguishable on the interior. It was opened in August 1930, bringing the total working floorspace to 954,000 square feet, or 22 acres. An enlarged and improved Harding Hall was dedicated in 1930, with raised ceilings, a seating capacity of 1,800, and a full-size, fully-rigged stage. The dedication was attended by Members of Congress, printing industry officials, the Librarian of Congress, the type designer Frederick W. Goudy, and Maj. Thomas Defrees, the son of Lincoln's Superintendent of Public Printing, John D. Defrees. Meanwhile, though Carter continued to press for the replacement of the original Wendell building and its many additions, it would take another decade for Congress to act.

The construction of Building 2 in 1927 or 1928. The camera is probably on the Massachusetts Avenue sidewalk, between the corner of G Street and the Gales School.

Further renovations in 1930 raised the roof of Harding Hall to create a modern auditorium with a fully-rigged stage, balcony, and projection booth.

The Division of Planning brought order and efficiency to the writing of job specifications.

Public Printer Carter created a retail bookstore for Government documents in the 1896 annex building on H Street NW. It later moved to the front of Building 1.

TREES AND TRAINS

December is almost universally seen as "the holiday season" with special meanings for different groups and individuals. At the Government Printing Office there is no surer sign of that season than the appearance of a tree and trains in Harding Hall. Since 1922, this holiday display and other programs, parties, and charity drives have lent a festive air to GPO at year's end.

The tree and trains have been a part of the Office's history for almost as long as there has been a Harding Hall. The first Office activity held in the hall was on Christmas Eve, 1921. The following year brought the first formal holiday program on December 22, 1922, when the GPO Orchestra played music for both day and night employees, and over 1,500 children enjoyed a "Christmas Entertainment" sponsored by the Cafeteria and Recreation Association.

By 1923 there were printed programs for the holiday events. The Orchestra played an overture, followed by marionettes, an "Our Gang" comedy, trained pigeons, a parade of wooden soldiers, and a playlet set in Santa's workshop. The parade and playlet were performed by pupils of Miss Cora Shreve's Dancing Academy. The program was given twice, on December 28 and 29 (although the record is silent on the omission of the trained pigeons from the second performance).

Through the 1920s and 1930s the programs grew. Jugglers, dancers, ventriloquists, and ballerinas added their talents to the Orchestra's renditions of "Jingle Bells" and other holiday songs. The increasingly elaborate programs were funded by the Cafeteria and Recreation Association through such projects as its candy sale, which in 1925 sold more than 5,000 pounds of candy to defray holiday expenses.

Even the Depression did not dampen the annual celebration. In 1933, 2,600 children each got a free show, a present, cake, and ice cream. The holiday open houses for families continue, although in less elaborate form, to the present.

Harding Hall grew and trees and trains grew larger and more lavish. This photo is from the 1940s.

In 1973 the traditional holiday celebration became a community open house, inviting local youngsters and their families for a look at the train, a visit with Santa, and refreshments. This is from the second open house, in 1974.

In the 1970s, GPO began to sponsor Community Day in December, inviting children from the surrounding community to share in the good cheer.

Unchanging, however, are the tree and trains, which are shown in photographs dating to the 1920s. The earliest shows a rather stumpy tree (by later standards), dwarfed by the low-built ceiling of old Harding Hall. A portrait of President Harding probably indicates that the photo is from 1922. The trains shown are real collector's items, probably "O" gauge. As years passed, trees grew larger and more elaborate, as did the train layout. Great care and pride continues to be lavished on this annual GPO tradition by GPO's electricians and carpenters.

The apprentice training program grew in the 1920s, with congressional authorization for 225 apprentices. This is the class of 1923.

APPRENTICESHIP

Apprentices were trained at GPO from its earliest days. In the late 1880s, apprentices spent four years learning their trade. Unlike the later program, no arrangement was made for keeping these workers. In 1895, Congress authorized the Public Printer to appoint no more than 25 apprentices, but successive agency heads did not use this authority, leaving the Office with no apprentices at all.

This situation began to change with the appointment of Public Printer Carter. In 1922, 162 applicants, all male, took an examination and 118 qualified for appointment to the 25 slots. Carter also stressed the need to utilize World War I veterans. Every person accepted into the program was guaranteed a journeyman position upon graduation.

Apprentices in the 1920s and 1930s undertook a four-year training program under the supervision of master craftsmen. After 1925, grammar, spelling, math, and printing history were taught in-house. In 1923, the ceiling on apprentice appointments was raised to 200, with new classes entering GPO every year. GPO included at least a few African-Americans in the program. In 1935, the first woman graduated from the apprentice school as a compositor.

Apprentices had classroom instruction as well practical experience in the various working sections.

The coming of the Depression put an end to new apprentice classes from 1931 to 1935, when 100 were selected. The term was increased from four to five years, with more academic courses added to training in the traditional craft skills. These classes also did a great deal of practical work and fine printing.

World War II saw another suspension of new apprentice classes until 1947 when one more class, composed solely of veterans, entered GPO. In 1956, 50 apprentices began a new era in training, and in 1969 the apprentice ceiling was raised to 400 and the program reduced to four years. From 1970 on, half of each class was drawn from within GPO, allowing employees throughout the Office to enter the crafts. This move also increased minority representation.

In 1974, due to the impact of electronic photocomposition, GPO offered retraining to affected employees, effectively eliminating the need for most apprenticeships. After 1975, the apprentice program began to operate in much lower gear to accommodate the reduced demand for trained personnel in traditional fields.

The long history of GPO's apprentice program shows both the Office's commitment to quality training for its employees and an ability to adapt to changing technology and social conditions.

The apprentice program as expanded in the 1920s was open to women and remained so until the program was suspended in World War II. Women began to be recruited again in the 1970s. Here an apprentice operates a Monotype keyboard.

The Kiess Act

Like other Public Printers before him, particularly Public Printer Ford, Carter worked hard to improve wages and in 1923 argued the necessity for system of pay better than the fixed rates still used by Congress:

> With the present wage scale as fixed by law it has been impossible to retain some of the best workers and to attract enough other properly skilled…[workers] to fill their places. During the year 269 printers, including 108 Linotype operators, 64 compositors, 23 monotype keyboard operators, and 44 proofreaders, left the service of the Government Printing Office, some of them going reluctantly to accept higher wages offered elsewhere.

To remedy the wage system and ensure enough workers for GPO, Carter recommended that Congress give GPO employees the right to negotiate for their wages which was the system used in the private sector. The passage of Public Law 276 on June 7, 1924, provided the system Carter was looking for. Known as the Kiess Act after its sponsor, Representative Edgar Kiess of Pennsylvania, the new law authorized the Public Printer to establish rates of pay based on collective bargaining with employees organized by the trades. Carter reported:

> Much credit is due to the Senate and House Printing Committees for the success of their endeavor to end the ancient practice of Congress to fix the pay of…[the crafts] at long and irregular intervals, and to establish instead a modern plan of collective wage bargaining. …The Kiess Act is the first formal recognition by Congress of the right of collective wage bargaining and arbitration with Government employees… [and] establishes also the principle of a minimum wage for certain trades. The act may therefore be deemed a landmark in labor legislation.

GPO historian Robert Kling said, "This law relieved Congress of the onerous and unfamiliar task of setting wages for the various crafts in the Office, and placed the…labor-management relationship between the head of the Office and the employees of each craft who were represented by democratically elected committeemen."[24] Wage negotiations between committees representing labor and management followed. Agreements were swiftly reached and approved by the Joint Committee on Printing. The pay of 3,800 employees was adjusted upward. At a meeting of 3,000 employees in Harding Hall on December 31, 1924, Carter was presented with a resolution of appreciation and thanks. The system of wage bargaining begun under Public Printer Carter continues to this day, affecting the wages of approximately three-quarters of GPO's workforce.

Along with the Kiess Act, another of Carter's contributions that was to influence the culture of the "big shop" for decades was his successful bid to restore and expand apprentice training. Congress had given authority to the Public Printer in the Printing Act of 1895 for the recruitment and training of a small number of apprentices. That authority was not accompanied by any mandate, however, and little was done. In the aftermath of World War I, Carter saw a need for a growing GPO to train its own journeymen printers and binders. He proposed the establishment of a formal apprentice program, which in addition to meeting GPO's staffing needs would provide the opportunity for war veterans to receive vocational training, including those then employed by GPO who had served in World War I, the Spanish-American War, and—even at that date—the 20 who had served in the Civil War. The JCP enthusiastically approved the program, observing "it is a good American doctrine to give the American boy a chance to learn a trade." The first apprentices were appointed in July 1922, and the program has continued, though changed in scope and duration, to the present day.

Carter also oversaw what would become one of GPO's most prominent product lines when, in 1926, GPO began producing passports for the State Department. The first U.S. passport was designed and produced by Benjamin Franklin in Paris while he was a delegate to the conference preparing the treaty granting American independence. The document he produced was a pass to enter the United States, identifying the bearer as a trusted individual who could move freely between America and other nations. In the early years of the Republic, an official passport could be obtained with a letter from virtually any city or state official, notary public, or justice of the peace. In 1856, the State Department established centralized control of passport applications and issuance, and the job of producing

Apprentices learning hand composition, 1939.

Apprentices learning page makeup and imposing.

An apprentice in the Press Division, 1939.

Apprentices running job presses in the Apprentice School, which produced most of GPO's internal printing, including notices, menus, newsletters, and programs.

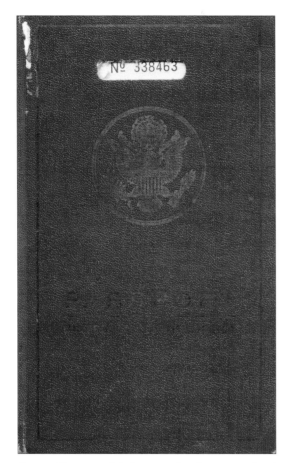
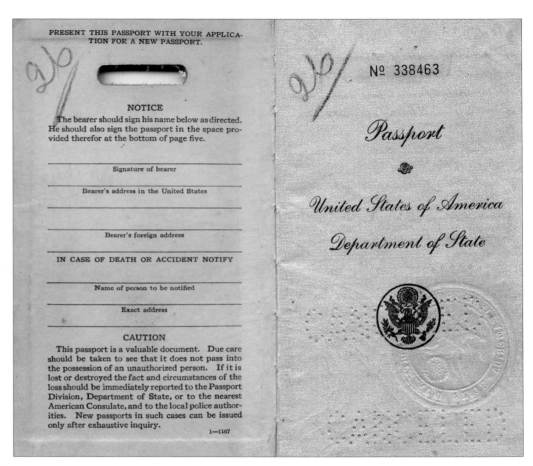

Cover and inner page of the first generation of passports produced at GPO.

passports—at that time a single engraved page—was given to the Treasury Department's Bureau of Engraving and Printing. In the 1920s, the League of Nations created an international standard for a booklet-style passport. The standard established passport size, number of pages, and other aspects of its design. Subsequently, the work was given to GPO, which has produced U.S. passports ever since.

It was not only on the printing side of the house that Carter was an innovator. Criticism had long been directed at the Government for alleged waste in the distribution of public documents. While the Printing Act of 1895 had transferred the Superintendent of Documents to GPO, by the

1920s the mechanism for libraries to actually receive materials was an ongoing frustration to librarians and GPO alike. Libraries were expected to receive and make available whatever GPO sent them, and to keep it indefinitely. At Carter's suggestion, Congress enacted a bill in 1922 directing that no part of the appropriation for document distribution to libraries could be used to supply documents to libraries that the libraries had not requested. This principle of selectivity was put into practice with a system that allowed libraries to tell GPO which classes of documents they wanted to receive. The item number system that grew from this change continues to drive the distribution of printed documents today.

Public Printer Giegengack

Following the election of President Franklin D. Roosevelt in 1932, Public Printer Carter continued in his position. However, a novel campaign for the position was undertaken by Augustus E. Giegengack, of New York. Born in April 1890, Giegengack became a journeyman Linotype operator and served as a sergeant in World War I in France. He was supervisor of production for the *Stars and Stripes*, the serviceman's newspaper, which had a circulation of 550,000 and was printed in the Paris plant of the *London Daily Mail*.

Following Roosevelt's election, Giegengack became active in the New York Democratic Club and got the organization to write to the President-elect on his behalf. He got the club to invite the new Postmaster General, James A. Farley, to a testimonial dinner with Giegengack as chairman. He next formed an organization and had letterhead printed, "A. E. Giegengack for Public Printer, Graphic Arts Committee. Organized to secure the appointment of A. E. Giegengack as Public Printer of the United States." On that letterhead he solicited backing from printing groups and other supporters of the President. Eventually over 200 letters were bound in a large red and gold volume titled, "A. E. Giegengack for Public Printer, which was given to Postmaster General Farley for presentation to the President." Giegengack's campaign had the desired effect, and he was sworn into office in July 1934.[25]

Public Printer Giegengack, like Carter before him, made a great many changes to the GPO organization that would have lasting impact. He created a division of Typography and Design and reorganized the Layout Section of the Planning Division, "for the purpose of modernizing and improving the appearance of Government publications with the intent to create a greater demand. ..." With better appearance also came economy. A greater emphasis on simple, standardized layouts and typographic standards streamlined not only the look of publications but reduced the amount of expensive preparation, makeup, and presswork. These changes meant less expense for agencies. The average charge per page per thousand copies went from $2.11 in 1937 to $.93 in 1939.

Also like his predecessor, Giegengack took a keen interest in GPO employees. He encouraged the founding of veterans organizations, including an American Legion post and auxiliary and a post of the Veterans of Foreign Wars. By 1937, GPO's American Legion Post 3874 numbered

434 members, one of the largest in the District of Columbia. On September 21, 1937, the post and its band, marching with their charter member, the Public Printer, participated in a parade down New York's Fifth Avenue.

Group life insurance for GPO employees began in May 1931, followed in 1935 by the introduction of group hospitalization insurance. By 1939, 1,629 GPO employees were members, paying 65 cents a month for insurance that provided 21 days of hospital care in any District of Columbia hospital, with a 10% discount beyond the 21 days. The GPO Federal Credit

Augustus E. Giegengack, GPO's longest serving Public Printer, began his career as a Linotype operator before managing the production of Stars and Stripes *during World War I.*

"Mr. Public Printer," caricature of Giegengack in The New Yorker, *June 1943.*

PROFILES..THE
PUBLIC PRINTER.I...IN
THE NEW YORKER, JUNE 12, 1943

* * * * * * * * * * *

AUGUSTUS E. GIEGENGACK, the thirteenth Public Printer of the United States and a man who wears spats whenever the temperature falls below forty, is probably more responsible than any other one man for the paper shortage in this country. As head of the Government Printing Office, he runs an organization which uses up more than seven hundred tons of paper a day, enough for over two million copies of the New York *Times*. Ever since the Printing Office was modestly established in 1861, it has grown in scope until it now handles most of the printing and binding for the federal government. Last year, directly or by subcontract, it did a business of nearly $47,000,000; this year the figure will be in the neighborhood of $65,000,000. In 1934, when Giegengack became its chief, the Printing Office,

7

Union traces its origin to this period. In 1935, a charter was granted for the GPOFCU, which by 1939 had 2,972 members holding shares worth $192,483.28. Worker safety has loomed large as a concern throughout GPO's history. Public Printer Giegengack formed an Executive Advisory Safety Committee that was charged with coordinating safety practices, establishing shop safety committees, setting safety rules and regulations to be issued by the Public Printer, promoting awareness, and keeping records to conform with Labor Department regulations.

As his energetic campaign for Public Printer showed, Giegengack had a natural gift for public relations, nowhere more successfully deployed than in the three-part profile by Geoffrey T. Hellman which appeared in *The New Yorker* June 12, 19, and 26, 1943, under the title "Mr. Public Printer." This series—the only one of its kind for a Public Printer—closely tied Giegengack's outgoing personality with the work of the Office.

New Buildings for GPO

Like his predecessors, Giegengack focused on the inadequacies of GPO buildings, which still included the Wendell building dating to GPO's earliest days. In his first annual report in 1934, Giegengack noted that nearly a third of the area occupied by employees, equipment, and property was housed in old buildings. He said,

> too strong emphasis cannot be placed on the serious danger
> to the lives of employees from fire hazard, possible structural
> collapse of heavily loaded old wooden frame buildings, and
> from the use of antiquated elevators in these old buildings. …
> These conditions have reached a state of emergency where the
> Government should not further delay the demolition of danger-
> ous buildings. They should be replaced with a modern building
> to safeguard the lives of employees and to provide the space
> needed to meet present urgent needs for future normal growth.

His successful gambit was a case of pictures being worth a thousand words (and ultimately several million dollars). Giegengack hired a Washington commercial photographer to record the horrifying conditions in the accumulation of buildings that had grown like weeds around the original Wendell building, on the H Street side of the square. These he

Giegengack successfully petitioned Congress to raze the grab bag of structures that had grown up around the original Wendell building. This photo overlooks the H Street site, probably from the 8th floor of Building 2.

carefully captioned and bound for circulation on Capitol Hill to the Joint Committee on Printing, the Appropriations Committees, and others. The following year, in a similar introduction to the annual report but with the confident added heading "New Building Project," Giegengack wrote,

Building 4, on the east side of North Capitol Street between G Street and G Place NE. The building connects directly with the railroad by a bridge at the rear over 1st Street NE.

Two of the nine-foot high bas relief sculptures on the north side of Building 4.

With the hearty support of the chairman and members of the Joint Committee on Printing and the director of the Procurement Division of the Treasury Department, an initial appropriation of $2,000,000 [was made], with a total limit cost not to exceed $5,885,000…for necessary land and construction of annex buildings…including rights of way, furniture, moving expenses, rental of temporary quarters during construction, railroad sidings, alternatives to existing buildings, all necessary tunnels connecting proposed and existing buildings, demolition of existing structures, and all necessary mechanical equipment.

Progress was rapid. The first building to be constructed was a three story warehouse on the southeast corner of North Capitol Street and G Place NE, facing Building 1. Demolition of old buildings between North Capitol Street and 1st Street NE began in October 1936 and excavation started in November. The completed building, later dubbed Building 4, was linked with Union Station by a railway trestle to accommodate the delivery of paper shipped by rail; the paper was then taken through a tunnel 30 feet under North Capitol Street to GPO's production operations. Special congressional legislation was enacted to authorize the rail spur into the building. The new warehouse was turned over to the Public Printer in February 1938, at a cost of $184,367 for the site and $1,264,000 for the building. On its exterior, the Art Deco style building featured four bas-relief sculptures by sculptors Elliot Mens and Armin A. Scheler. James M. Goode, in his book *Outdoor Sculpture of Washington DC: A Comprehensive Historical Guide*, describes the sculptures:

Three low-relief panels, each approximately nine feet high by five feet wide, are placed at intervals along the third story of the building on the north side. …The left panel shows a printer at work. His muscular body, executed in flat, rectilinear planes, is contrasted with a design of wheels and belts suggesting a printing press. The center panel bears the seal of the Government Printing Office, with a printing press emblazoned on a vigorous cartouche guarded by an American eagle. The right panel…portrays a worker unloading rolls of

Public Printer Giegengack lays the cornerstone for Building 3 at the corner of North Capitol and H Streets NW, February 1939.

Building 3 at its completion in 1940.

newsprint. He is shown from the back, his left leg thrust powerfully forward as he lifts the heavy rolls.[26]

Across North Capitol Street, progress on the new building at the corner of H Street NW, on the site of the original Wendell building, was less swift. Bids for construction exceeded the funds appropriated. Giegengack was again persuasive, and the 75th Congress increased the total limit to $7,700,000, allowing contracts to be awarded in May 1938. Demolition of the old Wendell building, along with its multiple add-ons, began in June. In February 1939, at the cornerstone-laying ceremony for the new building, the Public Printer and other dignitaries buried a time capsule, a sealed copper box containing a Bible, a flag, photographs of President Roosevelt and Giegengack, annual reports, a roster of employees, current Washington, DC, newspapers, and copies of various Government publications including the *Congressional Record* and the *Congressional Directory*.

Designed by Louis A. Simon, the new structure later dubbed Building 3 was occupied in early 1940 with a net floor area of 481,975

square feet. The building design and mass closely follow the pattern of the 1903 building, with eight stories, a façade on North Capitol Street of nearly equal width, complementary color of brick, and similar proportions and arrangement of windows. In place of the 1903 building's Romanesque detail, the 1940 building exhibits a spare Art Deco influence, the only decorative elements being the main entrance with stylized carved Art Deco eagles, and bronze lanterns flanking all entries. The final cost of the building was $5,026,000. With its completion, the total space occupied by GPO's four buildings was 1.5 million square feet, the equivalent of more than 34 acres. Most importantly, for the first time in many decades everyone in GPO worked in solid buildings that were not firetraps.

The *Federal Register*

Shortly after taking office, Giegengack helped to oversee the creation of the daily *Federal Register*, which along with the Congressional Record was to become a mainstay of GPO's workload. The need for the *Register* grew out of the increase in executive rules, regulations, bulletins, notices, and orders that accompanied the growth of the Federal Government beginning in the late 19th century, particularly with the establishment of independent regulatory agencies. The conditions under which these documents were promulgated, as well as their form and format, were anything but standardized.

The Federal Register began life in 1935, and has been published by the Office of the Federal Register and GPO every business day since.

With the advent of the New Deal, there was another explosion in these documents, and the situation grew increasingly chaotic. Writing in the *Harvard Law Review,* (later Dean of the Harvard Law School) Erwin Griswold noted, "in the first year of the National Recovery Administration, 2,998 administrative orders were issued…[and] numerous regulations and sets of regulations…are to be found scattered among 5,991 press releases during this period." The solution, argued Griswold, was "an official publication, analogous to the Statutes at Large, in which all rules and regulations shall be systematically and uniformly published," along the lines of the *Official U.S. Bulletin,* which was published as a sort of daily Government newspaper during World War I, published weekly thereafter for a brief period, and finally discontinued in the early 1920s. The need for the new publication crystallized in 1934 when Government attorneys found themselves prosecuting a case before the Supreme Court under an executive order that was no longer in effect.

In 1935, Congress enacted a law establishing the Division of the Federal Register within the new National Archives and providing for the daily publication of the *Federal Register* containing all proclamations, orders, rules, and regulations of the executive branch.[27] The Public Printer, along with the Archivist of the United States and a representative of the Attorney General, were appointed by law as the Administrative Committee of the Federal Register to oversee its publication. Subsequent legislation created the *Code of Federal Regulations*, and the Division of the Federal Register over the years was given responsibility for additional publications produced through GPO, including the *U.S. Government Manual*, *Public Papers of the Presidents*, and the *Weekly Compilation of Presidential Documents*. All of these documents became major products of GPO's in-house production operations, and with the exception of the *Weekly Compilation*, which now appears online as the *Daily Compilation of Presidential Documents*, continue to be produced by GPO today.

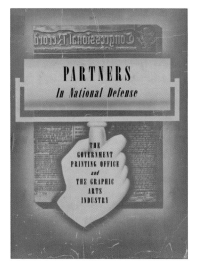

Public Printer Giegengack formed partnerships with the printing industry during World War II that set the stage for much of GPO's future. This booklet outlined his desire for cooperation during the national emergency.

World War II

As the United States approached World War II, GPO's plant employed 126 linecasting machines, 100 Monotype keyboards and 130 casters, and 202 presses ranging in size from small platen job presses to the giant web presses that produced the *Congressional Record* and the *Federal Register*. Printing orders associated with war mobilization activities had begun to flood GPO even before the Japanese attack on Pearl Harbor. By the end of 1941, the

Selective Service had already received 144,515,061 finished pieces, costing $286,164, which included the postcards and forms draftees began receiving in late 1940. The Treasury Department began a savings bond and stamp program that required 10,000,000 advertising folders, 931,000 four-color posters, and 20,000,000 stamp albums. By the time GPO printed in the *Congressional Record* President Roosevelt's famous "day of infamy" speech requesting a declaration of war, GPO had already taken steps to prepare for the coming emergency.

The most significant of these was the forging of a new partnership with the printing industry. It was clear to Giegengack from the outset that as extensive as GPO's capabilities were, the likely demand placed on the agency by wartime printing requirements would exceed its capacity. In March 1941, he called together a conference of leaders from the industry to discuss threats and agree on a course by which GPO would procure printing from the private sector. The Joint Committee on Printing agreed and in 1942 issued supplemental rules and regulations on the purchase of printing under provisions of the new War Powers Act. Giegengack's central aim was to organize GPO in such as way as to manage procurement, scheduling, and the control of equipment, paper, and other resources as if all work were taking place in the plant on North Capitol Street. In a report issued by GPO in 1947, *Public Printing in Peace and War*, Giegengack described this new "partnership between government and industry" which would reshape GPO permanently:

> The [printing industry] groups…collaborated in the preparation and distribution of a brochure on the subject of commercial cooperation in Government printing. An informal advisory committee of about 50 members, comprising printing trade association executives and other trade leaders…was organized. The effort was massive, beginning with an inventory of 4,000

The volume and variety of wartime printing during World War II was vast.

firms nationwide, to collect information on capacity, location, size of operation, and specifications. As the information was received it was coded, classified, and filed for reference as needed. …During the emergency, orders were placed with approximately 1,900 firms, many of which were granted only one order while others received hundreds. As the Office's experience widened, a range of contracting and planning practices were developed.

One of the key products of GPO's partnership with the printing industry during World War II was the series of colorful posters seeking recruits, advertising war bonds, warning against the inadvertent disclosure of war information, encouraging the salvaging of scrap and other materials for the war effort, and other purposes. The posters are one of the most enduring printing legacies of the war effort, and most of them were printed by contract printers who had color printing capabilities. The war also saw the production of a variety of unusual products reflecting the Nation's commitment to its armed forces, such as the words to popular songs and kits for the production of plays and shows that were printed and shipped to soldiers and sailors overseas. Additionally, the war effort drew on the talents of a host of writers and designers who were either well known at the time or would become so, including Theodore Seuss Geisel, later known to millions as Dr. Seuss, who wrote health pamphlets for the Army.

Giegengack's report on wartime printing also described the establishment of another emergency innovation, regional paper warehouses, to manage the necessary supply of paper and prevent shortages:

> …a publication to be distributed from the War Department depot at Ogden, Utah, might be printed in San Francisco. In

REPELLENTS

A repellent is just a 75 cent name for stuff to put on you that will keep *Ann* away.

This is Ann, Shes's Dying to Meet You, a booklet on preventing malaria, was illustrated by Theodore Geisel with text by Munro Leaf. Both were celebrated children's authors in their post-war careers.

such a case, it would be inefficient and costly to ship the paper for the job from the Printing Office in Washington. The establishment of local warehouses in printing centers near the largest distribution points maintained by the ordering agencies would enable us to procure and store paper nearby and have it quickly available at all times.

The functions of storekeeper, purchasing agent, and GPO technical liaison were combined in the duties of the managers of the warehouses, which were a wartime expedient. They were liquidated in December 1945.

The war was demanding on GPO's employees and its equipment. The 1939 volume of 6.5 billion printed copies amounting to $18.2 million soared to 22.8 billion copies in 1945, totaling $77.3 million. As it had during World War I, the plant worked around the clock and on extraordinary deadlines. Not only were the quantities and the schedules challenging, GPO took on a wide variety of unusual and innovative work during the war. Products were developed for special security needs such as special paper for ration coupons, soldier ballot paper, and prisoner of war stationery. Shortages of paper, ink, and most other basic materials had to be managed, often calling on the ingenuity of employees. In another realm, a wide assortment of quality projects were ordered through the war years, including printing for the United Nations Conference and the United Nations Charter in 1945, and President Roosevelt's citation for the people of Malta in 1943. Roosevelt, a knowledgeable bibliophile, could be a demanding customer, but was quick to acknowledge good work:

One of GPO's most exacting customers was President Roosevelt. During World War II he asked for this elaborate presentation of a citation for the people of Malta honoring their valor during the early part of the war.

I wish to congratulate you and your craftsmen on the splendid workmanship displayed on the scroll which was presented by me to the people of the Island of Malta. It was very beautifully done and I am sure we can all be proud of this product of our Government Printing Office. [signed] Franklin D. Roosevelt.

Of all the items sent to GPO for printing in World War II, one received unusually careful attention: War Department General Order 29, announcing the death and mourning of President Roosevelt in April 1945. As Giegengack later reported,

Copy of the order, to be printed on a black-bordered page 5 7/8 by 9, was received at 11:30 a.m. April 13. Type was set, proof submitted, and okayed proofs returned by the department by 12:35 p.m. In less than an hour 64 plates were processed by the foundry; the first of 16 of these were imposed on the press by 1:40 p.m., and all by 2:35 p.m. Four presses were used for the run. At 2:10 p.m. the first lot reached the bindery, where they were drilled with three holes and tied in packages of 500, and at 2:30 p.m. 1000 copies were delivered to the department. Successive deliveries were made during the next three hours… [the final] 134,000 at 5:30 p.m. The order required 1,010 pounds of paper and made 450 packages. …The entire quantity of 225,000 copies was printed and delivered within five hours.

Throughout the war, Giegengack worked to maintain employee morale, and to keep up the link between GPO and its employees who were serving in the armed forces. In a Christmas letter to employees serving abroad in 1944, the Public Printer said,

Don't hesitate to let those with whom you are associated in the service know that you are an employee of the Government Printing Office, as this Office has established a work record of which you, as an employee, can be justly proud. Your co-workers have printed and bound some of the most stupendous jobs in extremely short time. For fear of divulging military information I will not mention the names of any publications,

but you in the field have seen the imprint of the Government Printing Office in all stages of the fight from training manuals in camp to the bombing tables used over Berlin and Tokyo.

The war challenged GPO in a variety of ways, beginning with the problem of replacing productive workers who went off to serve. By V–J Day in 1945, 2,500 GPO employees had left for military service.

Nearly 2,500 GPO employees served in the armed forces in World War II, and of these, 63 were killed and 139 disabled. As servicemen and women began to return after the war, Giegengack established the position of Veteran's Coordinator to "insure a central and definitive authority and source of assistance for veterans with personalized service to each of them on return to duty." By 1947, 1,622 veterans had returned to work at GPO.

Public Printer Geigengack served until March 1948, a term of nearly 14 years, the longest in GPO history. Under his leadership, significant and lasting changes were made at GPO. He left GPO with two new, modern buildings and developed the work processes for major new product lines, including the *Federal Register*. Wartime work brought offset presses and printing to the forefront, valued for its speed and economy. Within a few years offset would supersede letterpress almost entirely. The wartime reorganization of the Office remained in place for many years, and after the war GPO absorbed several emergency printing plants established for executive agencies in Chicago, Denver, Seattle, New York, and at the Washington Navy Yard, which would continue as GPO organizations. Most significantly of all, the cooperative partnership between GPO and private printers established during the war set a pattern that would develop and expand to the present day.

Public Printer Deviny

Following Giegengack's resignation, President Truman appointed John J. Deviny as Public Printer in May 1948. Born in 1892, Deviny was a native

A big part of the war effort was keeping up morale. Here Harding Hall hosts a dance, raising spirits as well as promoting war bond sales.

INVISIBLE WRITING MADE VISIBLE

From late 1942 to mid-1946, the United States experienced an unprecedented influx of almost a half million German, Italian, and Japanese prisoners of war. They were in a position to damage the war effort through attempts at escape and, based on prior experiences in World War I with German prisoners of war, the possibility of espionage.

Since the Geneva Convention mandated that prisoners of war could write home, significant information on prisoners' locations and labor activities could be transmitted through the use of invisible inks made from such common substances as lemon juice, milk, washing soda, baking soda, starch solution, and even human urine. The War Department turned to GPO's paper chemists for an answer.

After extensive tests, GPO's experts developed a paper base with a silicate or clay coating. The coating contained a powder or dyestuff that would react to moisture or any acid water solution by turning green. The paper was called Sensicoat.

This paper's heavy 56-pound weight and high cost were negative factors, so GPO then developed a lighter, uncoated, and more economical paper, Analith.

After this paper went into production, secret messages to the Axis were greatly reduced. It was a reduction noticed and acted upon by German intelligence.

American censors noticed something very interesting about packages of food and clothing addressed to German prisoners as 1944 passed the halfway mark. A small amount of putty-like material about size of a kitchen match head began to turn up in various places of concealment. Repeated tests showed that the putty-like material was a dry ink.

After several conferences with the Bureau of Censorship regarding this problem, GPO's chemists began work on a new paper, bearing in mind that it also would have to retain its sensitivity to fluid invisible inks. The result was a coated sheet processed with a water-sensitive formula and with great sensitivity to the detection of all types of dry inks.

By 1945, more than 29 million sheets of the new stationery had been ordered at $1.04 per thousand and GPO had blocked a potentially dangerous flow of information to America's enemies. It was an achievement shrouded in wartime secrecy, but one gratefully acknowledged by those who knew about the technical difficulties involved.

(Northwestern University Libraries)

THE CHARTER FOR THE UNITED NATIONS

Early in 1945, the State Department requested that GPO provide the printing for the United Nations Conference in San Francisco. At that time, GPO's wartime San Francisco Warehouse had only five employees, so several additions were made to the staff and an emergency call went out to Washington for three key GPO central office employees. Until the Conference ended, this group carried out an incredible amount of rush work on an almost 24-hour a day schedule. Perhaps their most important job was the creation of the Charter establishing the United Nations

The last days of the conference saw the GPO unit racing against time and the oddities of Chinese and Russian typefaces to complete and deliver one of the Office's most momentous jobs.

GPO first found suitable printing paper. In addition to permanence, color, and weight, the paper needed to be "friendly" to writing inks because the charter would be signed by the assembled delegates. One hundred percent rag ledger paper most closely met these specifications, but there was not enough in the San Francisco area. An urgent message went out to the GPO central office in Washington and all available stock was shipped express to the West Coast.

Due to the nature of the written language, the Chinese type was handset. Because of last-minute changes, it proved necessary to reset about 40 pages of handwritten manuscript. In a frantic, all-night effort, several Chinese typesetters were pressed into service to handle this unexpected increase in the workload. The final crisis occurred when a pressman discovered that one character from a form was missing after printing six preliminary copies. The nearest extra characters were a mile away, so the Chinese translator checked

his proofs and an identical character was located on another page. The form was opened, the character removed and inked from the press ink roller, and then struck by hand into its proper place on all sheets which already had been run.

At the last minute, it was decided that an "e" rather than a "u" was needed on the last page of Russian text. The sole Russian typesetter was three miles away and there was no way that the job could be sent back and still meet the deadline. The GPO representative suggested that the Russian linotype lines be cut in two and a monotype English 'e' be inserted in its place between the cut portions of the slug.

(Northwestern University Libraries)

The English, Chinese, and Russian text sheets then joined the Spanish and French sheets at the University of California Press, where the signatures were folded carefully to avoid smudging the still-wet ink. Finally the charter was rushed to the Executive Secretary of the United Nations Conference on International Organization, who was waiting, with photographers, for the presentation ceremony.

So ended one of the most harrowing jobs ever undertaken by GPO. A handful of employees had planned and coordinated one of the most complex jobs ever to challenge the Office. Their only reward was a paycheck and the knowledge that they had contributed in a small way to international peace and understanding.

In 1953, the new Congressional Record *presses also revolutionized the printing of tax forms and instructions.*

Washingtonian who grew up in the neighborhood of GPO, graduating from neighboring Gonzaga College High School. After positions in private industry in the 1920s and 1930s, he served on the Social Security Board and became a member of the District of Columbia Bar. In 1941, he was appointed Deputy Public Printer under Giegengack.

Following his swearing-in Deviny observed, "I hope and expect to carry on the very successful policies and methods developed by my distinguished predecessor. …" His term was, in most respects, a continuation of his predecessor's. The U.S. involvement in the Korean conflict and the Government's civil defense initiatives created an upswing in printing in

the early 1950s. As GPO printed materials to train Americans to respond to military attack, the Office joined the effort in the District of Columbia, with shelter areas designated in all four buildings, drills conducted, and instruction in first aid and light rescue provided to employees.

After World War II, visitors again became a regular part of GPO life. When Building 3 opened, a convenient and comfortable room was included for the use of GPO's tour guides, who were typically members of the Apprentice School, and as a waiting room for visitors. In 1953, one official noted that, "in the past fiscal year we have had several visitors from abroad and also from our own country connected with the art of

John J. Deviny, Giegengack's deputy who succeeded him in 1948.

printing. In each instance, we were pleased with their remarks as to production, quality of work, cleanliness of our pressroom, and the orderly manner in which our…[work] is handled."

In 1949, Congress authorized the purchase of three large new web letterpresses for the production of the *Congressional Record*. Deviny confidently estimated that the new presses would cut costs and improve production. In 1953, the Production Manager reported that, "our experience with these machines to date indicates that the savings over the years will greatly exceed original estimates. This is made possible by the savings on income-tax printing which…is exceeding our original yearly estimate. …" That work came at the suggestion of Superintendent of Documents Roy Eastin, who in 1952 proposed to officials at the Internal Revenue Bureau a new package of income tax forms and instructions. After initial tests in selected cities, the tax package proved a significant saving because it could be entirely produced on the *Congressional Record* presses and wrapped as a self-mailer, rather than the older practice of various combinations of forms and instructions printed on various kinds of paper and on different presses, and then stuffed into envelopes. Approximately 48 million packages were produced in 1953 using the new presses, efficiently employing their capacity at times when they were not in demand for the *Record* and the *Federal Register*, and freeing other presses for smaller-scale work. The savings, both to GPO in paper, presswork, and bindery, and to the Internal Revenue Bureau in assembly and envelopes, were significant, totaling more than $625,000. This tremendous job took three months of production with all three *Record* presses running on two shifts, five days a week, a total of more than 33 million press impressions.

During Public Printer Deviny's term, Congress expanded the Joint Committee on Printing's authority over work produced elsewhere than GPO by enacting language empowering the Committee to approve the establishment of field, or agency, printing plants. Although President Truman approved the 1949 measure in order to avoid interrupting Government operations, he issued a statement echoing President Wilson's veto message by pointing out that the provision was "an invasion of rights of the executive branch by a legislative committee." He noted that many agencies were using duplicating equipment for the production of printing, and that because of recent regulations issued by the JCP defining duplicating equipment as printing equipment, the new law would bring duplicating processes operated by executive agencies under the control of Congress. President Truman called for a revision of Title 44 that would bring the printing statutes up to date, balance the proper roles of the executive and legislative branches in printing policy, and establish appropriate definitions for printed and duplicated materials. However, Congress did not take up the issue, and it was left to be resolved by subsequent generations.[28]

Public Printer Blattenberger

The 1952 election brought Dwight D. Eisenhower to the White House. Eisenhower looked for successful businessmen to direct Government agencies, and in 1953 he nominated Raymond Blattenberger to be Public Printer. A former printing company executive, Blattenberger was very clear about his brief from the White House: "What I'm trying to do is cut costs and run an efficient shop as economically as possible. …I didn't seek the job and I didn't want it. Now that I've got it, I'm going to concentrate first on saving money."

Raymond Blattenberger, who saw GPO through the McCarthy era.

In 1954, Blattenberger was able, through various modernization measures, to reduce GPO printing rates for agency work by 5%, the first reduction in 20 years. The following year saw salary increases for both craft and administrative employees. In 1953, the working capital appropriation established by Public Printer Carter became a revolving fund, and an annual budget was made part of the working landscape of the office. The offset and letterpress divisions were reorganized, and more efficient equipment was purchased. Blattenberger also oversaw the acquisition of modern typesetting machines. And, in what was described by a longtime GPO employee years later as the most significant improvement for employees, Office-wide air conditioning began to be installed in 1957, at a cost of $1.3 million.

GPO had been called the world's largest print shop since the turn of the 20th century, and it had steadily grown in capacity and production through two world wars and beyond. By the end of World War II, GPO was positioned for its last prolonged period of industrial growth. The demand for printed documents reached an all-time high during the war, and that demand continued into the prosperity of peacetime. The postwar GPO was organized around requirements for quick turnaround and large press runs. The established GPO ethos of self-sufficiency adapted itself to a growing operation. GPO's wartime expedient of buying printing from private sector printers became a permanent practice. From the 1950s to the 1970s, GPO kept pace with demand, particularly for agency publications, by augmenting its own plant capabilities with contracted printing. ❧

THE MCCARTHY HEARINGS

In August 1953, the Senate's Permanent Subcommittee on Investigations, chaired by Senator Joseph McCarthy, led an investigation of GPO. Hearings before the Subcommittee were conducted largely in closed executive session and the transcripts of the proceedings, totaling more than 175 pages, were not released by the Senate until 2003. On the basis of testimony provided by an FBI informant, the Subcommittee alleged that Edward Rothschild, a GPO bookbinder, had communist ties through his wife, who was not a Government employee, and that he had access to classified documents through GPO. Rothschild's attorney advised him to take the Fifth Amendment, and when he did, he was suspended from his job without pay. Rothschild was later discharged from Government service but never prosecuted. Other GPO employees who were identified as under security investigation were either suspended or transferred to the Library of Congress until their security cases were reevaluated, but none were prosecuted.[29] Although the hearings generated sensational headlines in the local newspapers that August, they failed to disclose any criminal breaches of security in the handling of Government documents at GPO, and by September the Subcommittee had moved on to other targets. Later that year, Blattenberger, who along with other GPO officials had testified before the Subcommittee and agreed to changes in GPO's security and loyalty programs, commented on the episode in a speech before the Printing Industry Association: "I want to say here and now that my experience has been that the vast majority of Government employees are loyal, hardworking citizens. …I must confess that my respect for the Government employee has greatly increased over the last five months."

IDENTIFIED AS COMMUNIST WORKERS—Mr. and Mrs. Edward Rothschild leave Senate Investigations Subcommittee hearing, where they were accused yesterday of being Communist workers.

JAMES PHILLIPS, Witness from GPO.

FREDERICK SILLERS, Jr. Refused to answer.

1960-1990

CHAPTER 4

EXPANSION AND COMPUTERIZATION

The 1960s ushered in an era of unprecedented social, political, and cultural change in the United States, as Congress and the administrations of Presidents Kennedy and Johnson enacted sweeping legislation affecting civil rights, education, poverty, conservation and beautification, space exploration, the environment and the arts, and other public policy areas. Over the course of the decade, GPO's volume of business doubled, and by the early 1970s GPO employment rose to its high water mark of 8,572, more people—including more minorities and women—than the agency had ever employed. But the way GPO carried out its work began to change fundamentally during this era, with the introduction of computers into the "big shop's" typesetting operations, and the increasing automation of other business and support functions. These and other changes begun in the 1960s, including increased printing procurement, the expansion of the depository library program, the explosion in documents sales, and growing diversity in GPO's workforce, continued through the 1970s and into the 1980s. With the final closeout of hot metal typesetting in 1985, GPO marked the end of an era and moved into a period of technological and organizational transformation.

James L. Harrison, like George Carter, had served on the Joint Committee on Printing before coming to GPO. He was appointed by President Kennedy in 1961.

Public Printer Harrison

The man who led GPO through the 1960s was James L. Harrison, who served as Public Printer from 1961 to 1970. At the time he was nominated by President Kennedy in March 1961, Harrison had been the staff director of the Joint Committee on Printing for a dozen years, which, like Public Printer Carter, provided him with invaluable experience with GPO. He had worked closely with Public Printers Deviny and Blattenberger and was familiar with the opportunities and problems the agency faced.

Harrison arrived at GPO just as the agency prepared to mark its centennial with a banquet in Harding Hall and the publication of the original edition of *100 GPO Years*, the first official history of the agency. The banquet was held June 27, 1961. Guests included Members of Congress, representatives of printing industry organizations, and GPO employees, as well as Public Printers Giegengack and Blattenberger, the widow of Public Printer Deviny, the daughter of Public Printer Carter, and the great-granddaughter of GPO's first executive, John D. Defrees. Other guests included the two oldest living GPO retirees. *100 GPO Years* appeared in June 1961. Several histories of GPO had been published previously but none was an official GPO publication. Although credited to the 100th Anniversary Committee established by Public Printer Harrison, the

Public Printer Harrison shows the new Consumer Information Center catalog to the First Lady, Lady Bird Johnson, with Presidential Assistant for Consumer Affairs Esther Peterson looking on. GPO has managed distribution of CIC publications since 1970 from its distribution facility in Pueblo, Colorado.

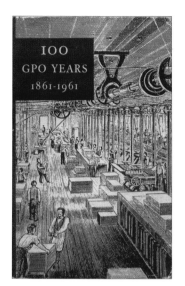

GPO published its first official history, 100 GPO Years, *in 1961, for the centennial of the agency's founding. Written by a self-described team of "ghosts," the principal writer and researcher was Harry Schecter, the chairman of the GPO Style Board.*

principal researcher, writer, and editor was Harry Schecter, Chairman of the GPO Style Board. The book was distributed free to all current employees and to depository libraries, and was also offered for sale by GPO.

Like Public Printers Carter and Giegengack before him, Harrison was an effective representative of GPO to Congress, Federal agencies, and the trade and mainstream press, and he kept in close touch with GPO's employees. *Typeline*, the GPO employee newsletter that continues to this day, began in May 1968 to inform employees of matters affecting them. It appeared every two weeks and was mailed to employees' homes (until 1972, when such mailings were discontinued as an economy measure). Other items included were announcements of training opportunities, new personnel policies and programs, new equipment acquired, new processes introduced, organizational changes, progress reports on charity drives, bond programs, and other GPO-wide programs. Special events such as the holiday open house and news of important visitors were also included. An employee contest was held to determine the permanent name of the publication. The winning entry was submitted independently by two employees, and each won a suggestion award of $25.

Harrison's connection with employees was critically important during the 1960s, as GPO's workload more than doubled, with revenues growing from $99.5 million in 1960 to $203.7 million in 1969. The value of congressional work alone rose from $11.5 million in 1960 to $31 million by the end of the decade. While some of these increases were due to inflation, the majority was the result of growth in volume. The number of original pages for regular publications such as the *Congressional Record*, congressional hearings, and bills grew, as did the page count for the *Federal Register*, rising

GPO's employee newsletter Typeline *began in 1968. The title was chosen in a contest among employees.*

by nearly 55% over the decade. Overall, requisitions and print orders rose from slightly more than 100,000 in 1960 to nearly 365,000 in 1969. An increased amount of work was sent to the commercial sector for production, rising from $35.6 million in 1960 to $103 million by the end of the decade. During this period, total GPO employment grew from 6,457 in 1960 to 7,971 by 1969.

Part of GPO's increased workload during the 1960s was the result of actions by the JCP to redirect printing work being handled by Federal agencies themselves to GPO for procurement from the private sector printing industry. The objective was to re-establish GPO as the Government's primary resource for printing, and by extension, public access to Government publications through the Superintendent of Documents. Under this policy, the share of work commercially procured by GPO increased dramatically from about a third in the early 1960s to nearly three-quarters two decades later. In 1970 GPO established a specialized procurement function focusing solely on printing and expanded the number of GPO printing procurement offices nationwide. Beginning with the creation in the late 1960s of procurement offices in St. Louis, Boston, and Philadelphia, GPO followed by setting up offices in Atlanta, Chicago, Columbus, Dallas, Denver, Hampton, VA, Los Angeles, New York, San Francisco, and Seattle, and at the Navy Yard in Washington, DC.

Search for a New Building

With GPO's burgeoning workload, the dominant issue for Public Printer Harrison during his term of office was an effort to move from GPO's buildings into larger, more modern space. By 1961, GPO's existing multistory facilities, which required paper and materials movements over

THE WARREN REPORT

Perhaps the single most important job of the 1960s was the *Report of the President's Commission on the Assassination of President Kennedy*, known as the Warren Commission Report, named after the Commission's Chairman, Supreme Court Chief Justice Earl Warren. Issued in 1964, the complete report comprised approximately 19,200 pages overall in 26 volumes of hearings averaging 400 to 500 pages each. These were released in November 1964, while the report itself, a volume of 900 pages, was released in September 1964 and was widely reprinted commercially. All the official GPO volumes were covered in blue cloth and stamped in gold and contained approximately 9,000 illustrations, including the first public release of still images from the Zapruder film of the assassination.

President Lyndon Johnson is presented with the report of the Warren Commission on the assassination of John F. Kennedy, by Chief Justice Earl Warren.

The report was designed by GPO's Typography and Design Division. Special security measures were set up by GPO to prevent unauthorized disclosure of the manuscript, including the use of internal monitors to oversee the entire production process for the final report. When a leak of one part of the report did occur, a subsequent investigation concluded that it did not come from within GPO, and in commenting on the matter, the Associated Press said, "The Printing Office has an impeccable reputation of preventing leaks on secret Government documents and advance leaks on publications with future release dates." [30]

---

different floors, were considered outmoded and increasingly cramped as workload and the workforce grew in size. Efforts to alleviate space shortages at GPO began during the preceding decade when the JCP directed a study of expanding GPO's paper warehouse in lieu of continuing to store paper at a leased facility in Franconia, VA. The study was submitted to the General Accounting Office, and the GAO concurred with its recommendation to construct an annex of three or four stories attached to GPO's Building 3, along H Street. The plan was approved by the JCP. Subsequently, Congress provided authority for the work and $6.5 million for site acquisition and construction.

Before the work began, however, discussions with the District of Columbia and the National Capital Planning Commission in 1962 sug-

gested that sites might be available within the District for a new GPO building. A new, larger, in-line production facility of up to two million square feet would remedy space constraints as well as the problems and costs of moving paper and materials in a multistory building and was seen as a better solution than construction of an annex. With JCP approval for a new building within thirty minutes of the Capitol, constructed on one level, and in a location served by rail for paper deliveries and shipment of finished product, GPO returned the funds for an annex to the Treasury and in 1964 obtained approval from the House and Senate Public Works Committees for a new building, at a projected cost of $46.7 million.

After fending off a challenge from the printing industry to the concept of a new facility, GPO's efforts then turned to finding a suitable site. Of the limited number available, one—at the Bolling Air Force Base in southeast Washington—was removed from consideration when the Defense Department refused to release it for development. Another, at the former National Training School for Boys site at Fort Lincoln, in northeast Washington, was removed from consideration as the result of local opposition that culminated in withdrawal of the property by the National Capital Planning Commission. GPO then turned to a site near the intersection of U.S. Route 50 and the Capital Beltway, in Prince Georges County, MD. Although approved by the JCP, this site was also removed from consideration as the result of opposition to the departure of GPO from the District of Columbia. Two other sites subsequently materialized in the District, one called the Harmony Cemetery site, near the present day Rhode Island Avenue/Brentwood Metro Station, and the other, the coal yard site on 1st Street, NE. However, neither was considered large enough for GPO's plans, and by the end of Harrison's tenure in 1971, GPO's relocation plans had ground to a halt.[31]

Development of the Linotron

More successful was GPO's initial foray into computerized typesetting. By the early 1960s, an increasing amount of work coming to GPO arrived as computer printout copy. Manuscript in this format contained information all in capital letters with the letters widely spaced, and resulted in bulky publications that were difficult to read. Even by photographically reducing the pages as much as possible, the volume generated by computer printout copy was staggering and costly. Thousands of computers then in use in the Federal Government held a significant amount of information, such as the results of Federally-funded research and development, which was not being printed and made available to the public because of the high cost of composition. In 1962, the JCP ordered GPO to come up with a remedy.

In 1964 the Mergenthaler Co. and CBS Laboratories won a GPO contract to build a machine called the Linotron. The Linotron took a computer magnetic tape from the publishing agency that had been programmed through GPO's computers, and composed the data in 6-point type at the rate of a page every 10 to 12 seconds, up to 1,000 characters per second, justified including upper and lower case letters, resulting in a page negative made up and ready to be plated and printed. The first Linotron went into operation in October 1967 and the second a year later. The re-

Senator Carl Hayden, dean of the Senate and longtime Chair of the Joint Committee on Printing (center), dedicates the Linotron with Public Printer Harrison (left), and Jack Haley, JCP staff director (right).

duction in publication bulk was estimated to average 40 to 50%. Keyboard production time internally was reduced dramatically. The dean of the Senate and Chair of the JCP, Senator Carl Hayden of Arizona, pressed the key starting the Linotron 1010 on its first job, the *Federal Supply Catalog*. The Linotrons cost $2.3 million to develop and install. In the first 13 months of operation the savings were estimated at $900,000. The introduction of the Linotron was characterized by Harrison as "the most important development in composition since the introduction of the Linotype machine at the turn of the century." With it, "it can truly be said that in 1968 the Government Printing Office entered the electronic printing age."

GPO launched itself into the computer age with the Linotron, a magnetic tape typesetting system developed under a GPO contract by the Mergenthaler Co. and CBS Laboratories.

Expansion of Public Access

In August 1962, Congress enacted the most significant legislative revision of the depository library program since the passage of the Printing Act of 1895. Provisions of the Depository Library Act of 1962 significantly expanded the scope of publications distributed to depository libraries to include documents printed in agency plants. The act also created the system of regional depository libraries—up to two per state—to provide for permanent public access to all publications distributed by the program, while allowing other selective depository libraries to discard their publications after five years. In addition, among other changes, the act revised the formula for depository designation. Although it stirred controversy during deliberations with GPO (among others) noting the costs and administrative burdens of assuming the new functions, the Depository Library Act set the pattern for the Federal depository library program that has survived to the present day.

The immediate effect of the new law was a dramatic growth in the number of participating libraries, rising from 592 in 1962 to 993 by the end of the decade, and in the number of publications distributed to the libraries, which more than doubled during the same period, from 5.3 million to 10.8 million. Congressional appropriations also increased, as reflected in the increase of the Superintendent of Documents Salaries and Expenses Appropriation from $4.7 million at the time of the act's passage to $8.2 million in 1969. This pattern of growth continued over the next two decades. As a result, the program became one the most prominent symbols of the Government's commitment to keep the public informed.

Along with the expanded distribution of Government documents to depository libraries came increased public demand for publications sales, with the issuance of noteworthy publications like the *Warren Commission Report* on the assassination of President Kennedy and the landmark 1964 Surgeon General's report on the dangers of smoking, as well as the myriad of other publications being issued by Federal agencies. During this period, income from publication sales nearly doubled, from $10.9 million in 1960 to $20 million by 1969, with the number of publications sold annually rising from 54.7 million to 71.5 million by the end of the decade.

To accommodate this demand, GPO began opening retail bookstores around the Nation, beginning in 1967 with two experimental outlets in Chicago and Kansas City, Missouri. Additional bookstores were opened in San Francisco in 1969 along with outlets in Washington, DC, at the State Department and other agencies. By 1975, GPO had six bookstores in the District of Columbia (at the main GPO, Commerce, the Pentagon, the United States Information Agency, State, and in the Forrestal building) and 19 other stores nationwide (Chicago, Kansas City, San Francisco, Boston, Los Angeles, Atlanta, Dallas, New York, Denver, Pueblo, Colorado, Birmingham, Canton, Ohio—later moved to Columbus—Detroit, Philadelphia, Cleveland, Seattle, Milwaukee, and Jacksonville). Two regional distribution centers were also set up in Pueblo, CO (following a proposal by Representative Frank Evans of Colorado, for whom the facility was named by an act of Congress in 2010), and Philadelphia. These were to reduce turnaround time in filling orders and provide more storage space for publications.

Public Printer Harrison ensured that GPO participated in the New York World's Fair that opened on April 22, 1964, in Flushing Meadows Park, Queens, NY, for a two-season run. An exhibit of Government publications was held at the Fair, prepared by GPO's Documents and Typography and Design personnel. The exhibit was housed in the United States Pavilion, highlighting select Government publications grouped by subject area. A general information leaflet about the publications and a listing of those on display at the Fair were specially prepared for distribution to interested visitors by the librarians in charge of the reference desks in the U.S. Pavilion. In addition to Government documents, fairgoers could see the newly introduced Ford Mustang, sample newly invented Belgian waffles, and see Walt Disney's "It's a Small World" attraction.

Best-Sellers: Humble and Historic

Since opening its doors in 1861, GPO has played a part in many of the most important events in American life, printing declarations of war and proclamations of peace, reporting landmark decisions and history-making legislation. But every working day since 1861, between those peak moments that history remembers, GPO has printed and distributed an unbroken stream of more modest documents that in themselves are a distinctive part of Americans' interaction with their Government.

Most Government agencies have in their fundamental charge the responsibility to communicate with the people. From the most general annual report to the most technical results of research, from little pamphlets to ponderous tomes, Government agencies create the message and GPO has provided the medium.

GPO has had many big sellers over the years, rising and falling on the tides of current events. Two publications of the more humble variety have a place in history for their unusual popularity and longevity. The Bureau of Animal Industry in the Department of Agriculture published *Special Report on Diseases of the Horse* in 1890. Over the next 52 years it would go through seven editions, and thousands of copies were sold by GPO as well as distributed by Members of Congress.

Perhaps the all-time bestseller was the pamphlet *Infant Care*, first published in 1914 by the newly established Children's Bureau. A GPO press release in November 1942 announced the 25,000,000th copy of *Infant Care*, and captured the significance of this type of Government document, "...in 1914 few mothers had access to authoritative information in low-cost form on the care of their babies." *Infant Care* remained an active best-seller through many more editions, the last in 1984. It was translated into eight languages and published in Braille.

As the Nation has grown and new media have multiplied, the amount of information widely available and the ease in obtaining it, the Government's role as a source of information has evolved as well. But GPO's part always has been, and will continue to be, played with jobs of historic importance in tandem with the present-day descendants of *Diseases of the Horse* and *Infant Care*.

GPO and Emergency Preparedness

Early in his term, Harrison directed GPO's emergency preparations when the Soviet Union's placement of offensive missiles in Cuba in October 1962 raised the specter of a nuclear confrontation. Like other Federal agencies, GPO took actions to ensure continuity of services in case the plant was incapacitated. Vital records, including personnel records, manuals, electronic tape programs, systems, rates, and related materials, were moved to a secure facility offsite. GPO made arrangements to purchase additional paper and materials to meet an expected increase in printing requirements, especially for defense agencies, and set up a program to train 60 printing procurement specialists to buy an increased volume of Federal printing

from commercial printers nationwide in the wake of an attack. The early civil defense efforts, now known as "continuity of operations" or COOP actions, were reactivated at GPO during the early 1980s and have become a fixture of GPO operational planning today.

The outbreak of rioting in Washington, DC, following the assassination of the Rev. Dr. Martin Luther King, Jr., on April 4, 1968, directly affected GPO. As disorder intensified on April 5 in the 14th Street NW and H Street NE corridors, many Federal employees—including GPO employees—left work early. A curfew that night by DC Police prevented many GPO nightside employees from reporting to work. As a result, for the first time in living memory GPO was unable to print the *Congressional*

Five days of civil unrest erupted following the assassination of the Rev. Dr. Martin Luther King on April 4, 1968. Curfews were imposed beginning April 5 that prevented night shift employees from reporting to work. GPO housed elements of Federal troups in Building 3.

By the late 1960s, the area around GPO had grown increasingly dangerous as the crime rate rose. In 1969, Harrison asked Congress to enact a law creating "special policemen" at GPO. These were to be officers selected, trained, and appointed by the Public Printer to "protect persons and property" at GPO. The policemen replaced the GPO guard force that had been in existence for many years, who legally had little more authority than any other private citizen to arrest and detain persons for violations of the law or GPO's regulations. The policemen were given specific authority to enforce the law, make arrests, and bear arms in carrying out these duties on GPO property and "adjacent areas." The House and Senate passed the bill in 1970 and it was signed into law. Today, GPO's uniformed police officers, supplemented by contract officers, continue to protect GPO's personnel and property.

Public Printer Spence

Following the election of President Richard M. Nixon in 1968, Harrison remained in office until 1970, when he was replaced by Adophus Nichols "Nick" Spence. Spence was a career Navy official who had managed printing services for the Navy and later the Defense Department, and had worked with GPO for many years in providing for the Department's printing needs, even testifying during the McCarthy hearings that to his knowledge there was no record of communist activity at GPO. Spence was a recognized authority on modern printing management and graphic communications techniques. At GPO, he introduced a number of management reforms and helped defuse a labor sick-out over a wage dispute that threatened to halt production of essential congressional work. Unfortunately, his tenure as Public Printer was brief; Spence died unexpectedly in January 1972, the only Public Printer to do so while in office.

Public Printer Spence came to GPO in 1970 from the Defense Department as President Nixon's appointee.

Federal troops stationed outside GPO Building 4 in April 1968.

Record. Curfews remained in effect every night until April 11, so GPO adjusted the work hours of night shift employees to arrive and depart from work before and after each curfew. During the crisis, Federal troops were posted at GPO facilities, including inside Building 3 and outside Building 4. In the months that followed, GPO—along with all Federal agencies—received policy guidance from the Civil Service Commission and the Justice Department to prepare for possible disturbances resulting from planned demonstrations, such as the Poor Peoples' Campaign in June 1968, and protests associated with opposition to the Vietnam War, including the Moratorium Days in October and November 1969 and the May Day protest in May 1971. These preparations helped ensure that GPO's work went on uninterrupted during this difficult period.

Public Printer McCormick

President Nixon appointed Thomas F. McCormick in March 1973. McCormick had spent his business career with the General Electric Company, eventually rising to be General Manager of the Maqua Company, a 400-employee printing firm owned by GE. During his tenure he joined the Printing Industry Association of Eastern-Central New York and served on its board of directors.

McCormick's first commitment was to continue the transition to computerized type-setting begun under Public Printer Harrison and urged on by the JCP. In 1974, GPO began upgrading its electronic photocomposition capability to capture keystrokes at their source. Agencies submitted data on magnetic tapes that were then passed through GPO's typesetting system to create formatted pages. None of this work required any keyboarding or proofreading at GPO; all data was captured, coded, and verified by customer agencies. By the mid-1970s, GPO was producing nearly half of its typeset pages using data captured at its source. The goal of electronic photocomposition then became the automatic composition of all work being performed at that time by hot metal composing techniques.

The first publications transferred were the daily *Federal Register*, the *Code of Federal Regulations*, and the *U.S. Code*, followed by the *Congressional Record*, all other congressional work, and the *U.S. Budget* publications. Coordination with congressional offices, the Office of the Federal Register, and other agencies led to the installation of components of an electronic compositon system in their offices. Type was set from key-strokes captured at the source rather than re-keyed by GPO. The result was a significant amount of work migrating to electronic photo-composition. By 1976, the number of pages photocomposed by GPO exceeded the number of pages composed on GPO's Linotype and Monotype machines.

To make this technology transition possible, GPO worked with the employees represented by the Columbia Typographical Union, Local 101, to retrain the workforce. The retraining resulted in providing workers with the skills to operate the new technology while suggestions from

Thomas F. McCormick, who followed Public Printer Spence in 1973.

workers benefitted the development of the new photocomposition system. The result was that GPO made the transition with the cooperation of labor and a minimum of occupational dislocation, unlike in other areas of the printing and publishing industry undergoing the same changes.

Building Expansion Plans

During his brief tenure, Public Printer Spence had advocated constructing an annex of 1.3 million square feet connected to the present buildings and extending westward toward 1st Street, almost doubling the current size of GPO. The new building would have three basement levels for parking and six stories above ground. It would face G Street NW, and the proposal included a plan to reface existing Buildings 1, 2, and 3 to look like the new structure.

In 1973, however, the National Capital Planning Commission recommended relocating GPO to Northeast Washington. Public Printer McCormick enthusiastically endorsed the plan. The location, known as the Brentwood site, was north of New York Avenue NW, near the present-day Rhode Island Avenue Metro station, with railroad access. The esti-mated construction cost was $158 million. The old GPO buildings would be turned over for other Government use, possibly by the General Services Administration (GSA) or the National Archives. Funding was provided for site acquisition and design and development of plans, and a detailed environmental impact study with community input was completed. However, in spite of continued efforts by Public Printer McCormick and the JCP, approval from Congress was not forthcoming and the site eventu-ally was occupied by the Postal Service in the early 1980s.

Without expanded space to move into, congestion in the main buildings during the 1970s was relieved by leasing space elsewhere. GPO continued to lease a paper warehouse from GSA in Franconia, VA, and moved this operation to a warehouse and office space in Springfield, VA, later in the decade. In 1974, GPO's depository library functions were moved to a warehouse in Alexandria, VA. The following year, the fourth and fifth floors of Union Center Plaza—commercial space located a block north of GPO on North Capitol Street—were leased and occupied by the Superintendent of Documents and GPO's newly formed Data Systems Service. Publications storage and sales fulfillment functions were moved to a 180,000 square foot warehouse in Laurel, MD, that same year.

Equal Employment Opportunity at GPO

In 1969, President Nixon signed an executive order mandating equal employment opportunity activities in Federal agencies. An outgrowth of this directive was the appointment of GPO's first Equal Employment Opportunity Officer and the beginning of EEO counseling services. In 1971, GPO's first Federal Women's Program Coordinator was appointed, and in 1973 an Hispanic Program Coordinator also became a part of EEO. In 1973, the EEO office sponsored a "Community Children's Day" for 350 local children, an event which subsequently became a traditional part of GPO's annual Christmas Program.

Against this backdrop, the 1970s saw two major court cases that opened doors to equal opportunity for GPO employees. Both helped form the body of law protecting all Federal employees from discrimination today.

Dorothy Thompson, 58-year-old grandmother who had worked in binderies for 33 years, was the lead plaintiff in a 1973 class action suit brought by more than 300 women bindery workers against GPO. They alleged that male bookbinders received greater pay than female bindery workers performing similar work and that as women they were denied access to bookbinder and supervisory positions. GPO argued that the difference in pay was based on "traditional industry patterns of classification and training" and therefore was based on a factor other than sex. The U.S. District Court did not agree, holding that GPO's separate classification system for bookbinder and journeyman bindery worker jobs perpetuated the effect of past sex discrimination, was not justified for business purposes, and violated Title VII of the Civil Rights Act of 1964. In his decision the District Court judge ordered the Government to pay an estimated $16 million to the women involved in the suit, which at that time, according to the *Washington Post*, was "one of the largest awards ever made in a bias case brought against an employer, public or private." Thompson said, "For years they told me the big industrial sewing machine I operate was women's work. But I knew all along I was doing a job same as men, but not getting paid the same."

Dorothy Thompson, lead plaintiff in a 1973 class action suit that won pay equity for women.

Alfred McKenzie was a GPO offset press operator who was a veteran of World War II as part of the famed Tuskegee Airmen unit. McKenzie was the lead plantiff in a 1973 class action suit brought by black employees of GPO's Offset Printing Section alleging racial discrimination. The plaintiffs claimed that GPO failed to hire, train, or promote black employees within the section. The case was noteworthy for producing the first decision in the District of Columbia based almost entirely on the use of statistical evidence. In 1977, the Court used this evidence to find "a sufficient showing by clear and convincing evidence that black employees in the Offset Press Section are and have been the constant target of racial discrimination and have been wrongfully denied equal opportunities in both employment and promotion." It took several more years before a final settlement was reached in the case, with a $2.4 million settlement in 1987 affecting more than 350 current and former offset press workers. McKenzie himself retired in 1973 and never saw a promotion, but he told the *Washington Post* the suit was well worth the effort. "I never had any idea it would turn out as large as it did," he said. "But as things started to develop I saw the chance to really help others. What made it worth the effort were the changes that have been made at GPO that are helping the workers there now."

Alfred McKenzie, who was lead plantiff in a class action suit in 1973 that addressed race discrimination in GPO's promotion and training practices.

Public Printer Boyle

Public Printer McCormick served through the administration of President Gerald R. Ford. Following his election in 1976, President Jimmy Carter accepted McCormick's resignation and appointed John J. Boyle as Public Printer in November 1977. Boyle's GPO career began in 1952 as a proofreader, and his technology and management capabilities, especially in the area of computerized typesetting, moved him up through the ranks. In

Some "Firsts" For GPO Women

W omen have always made their mark at the U. S. Government Printing Office. Through the years, they have risen to the challenge of being "firsts," whether in craft, administrative, or recreational work.

An early "first" woman at GPO was Adelaide R. Hasse. In 1895 she became the Office's first librarian, serving until 1897 and creating the system of documents classification still in use today.

In 1906 the production area produced another pioneer. Anna C. Wilson of the composing division became the first member of her International Typographical Union local to be named a delegate to the union's national convention.

After the First World War, women advanced further at GPO. In his 1922 annual report, Public Printer George H. Carter said, "Little or no recognition had been accorded the ability and industry of women workers in this office during all the past years. Accordingly, for the first time in the history of the office, several thoroughly competent women were advanced to suitable supervisory positions." Among those promoted were Josephine Adams (Assistant Superintendent of Documents), Martha Feehan (assistant foreman of the dayside proofroom), and Mary T. Spalding (foreman of the bindery sewing machine section). Carter also appointed Mary A. Tate as secretary to the Public Printer, the first woman ever to hold that post. Later, Tate was named Assistant to the Public Printer, specifically charged with overseeing all matters relating to women employees.

Another breakthrough came in 1931, when Blanche E. Boisvert and Beulah A. Fairell became the first women to participate in GPO's apprenticeship program. Boisvert went on to graduate from the program in 1935, another "first."

In 1931, Willa B. Dial became instructor of academic subjects in the apprentice school. This was not a "first" for women – that particular honor went to Pauline K. Dodge several years earlier. Dial's claim to pioneer status rests on being managing editor of GPO's first employee newsletter.

In 1942, the great wartime increase in plastic platemaking led the Superintendent of Platemaking to ask permission from the Public Printer to teach a woman the trade, so Gertrude Larson moved from the pamphlet bindery to begin her apprenticeship in platemaking.

African-American women faced many obstacles in those days. Although a trained soprano, Ethel M. Gray could not belong to GPO's choral group in the late 1930s because, like all Government agencies, GPO was racially segregated. She organized an African-American choral group – a 35-member organization that performed in GPO, over the radio, and at many churches, clubs, and wartime Red Cross benefits.

Since World War II women at GPO have continued to set and attain new goals for themselves in all areas of the Office. It would be an imposing task to list all of those achievements — such as Lois Schutte, GPO's first woman Director of Personnel, Judith Russell, first woman Superintendent of Documents, and Maria Robinson (Lefevre), first woman Chief of Staff. All of these pioneers have paved the way for others in GPO's increasingly diverse workforce.

John J. Boyle, nominated Public Printer by President Carter, had been Public Printer McCormick's deputy.

1973, McCormick named him Deputy Public Printer. Boyle was the first Public Printer to have risen from within GPO's own ranks. Like McCormick, his chief goal was ensuring the continued smooth transition to electronic photocomposition.

Boyle's term closed out the decade of the 1970s, a period when revenues rose from $259.3 million in 1970 to $701.5 million in 1979. Sales of publications increased to $44.4 million from $21.2 million. By the end of the decade, GPO procured nearly $426.6 million in products and services from the private sector printing industry, compared with $125.7 million in 1970. Persistent inflation throughout the decade, exacerbated by energy crises in 1973 and 1979, was responsible for a significant part of the increase in GPO's financial performance, as the purchasing power of the dollar sank by roughly half between 1970 and 1979. Nevertheless, the number of bookstores increased to 27 nationwide, with six in the District of Columbia alone. The number of bookstore customers rose from 379,300 in 1970 to more the 495,000 annually by the end of the period. By 1979, there were 14 regional printing procurement offices in operation nationwide, and the dollar volume of printing procured by GPO from the private sector had risen to more than 70% of all printing performed by GPO, compared with 59% a decade earlier. The number of Federal depository libraries grew from 1,033 to 1,329 by the decade's end, and the volume of publications distributed to the libraries nearly doubled.

Underneath that record of growth was a profound change in the way GPO did its work. As the end of the 1970s approached, the automation of printing systems as well as the expanding use of mainframe-based computer systems had begun to affect GPO, and had reduced GPO's overall employment level from its all-time high of 8,572 in 1972. Other changes in Government printing and distribution were underway. Paper issued for production and blank paper sales to other Federal agencies fell by nearly 42% during the 1970s, as GPO increased the level of procurement from the private sector, ended the practice of furnishing paper to commercial contractors, and began the use of microfiche for library distribution. In congressional printing, the JCP and the appropriations committees began trimming the number of documents produced, eliminating the semiweekly edition of the *Congressional Record*, and cutting the number of daily and bound *Record* copies that were printed daily by nearly a quarter. While the dollar volume of publications sales increased, the number of publications sold annually fell by nearly a third over the decade as GPO raised prices to cover rising postage costs and recover sales program costs. The signs of a coming change based on electronic information technologies were beginning to be seen.

In 1978, the JCP undertook a major effort to revise GPO's authorities under Title 44 because of technological advances that were changing the way Government publications were generated, produced, and disseminated. An Advisory Committee on the Revision of Title 44 was set up in late 1978. As a result of the Commission's work, a bill entitled the National Publications Act of 1979 was introduced and hearings were held. The bill would have repealed several existing sections of Title 44 covering Government printing, congressional printing and binding, sales of publications, depository library program, and abolished the JCP. GPO was to be replaced by a National Publications Office under the control of a Presidentially-appointed seven-member commission representing the printing industry, labor, and the library and information industry communities. The depository library program was to be expanded by providing Federal funding for equipment and training for libraries. The definition of "Government document" was to be expanded to included machine-readable data files and audio and visual presentations. However, the bill drew opposition when the Office of Management and Budget estimated the cost of enactment as high as $5 billion annually, and by 1980 the effort to move it forward in the legislative process was abandoned. Other Title 44 reform efforts would follow in the ensuing years.

Public Printer Sawyer and the JCP

Public Printer Boyle retired in early 1980, and in 1981 President Ronald W. Reagan appointed Danford L. Sawyer, Jr., as Public Printer. Sawyer had built a career in the advertising publishing business in Florida. He had been a long-time supporter of President Reagan, and he arrived at GPO committed to carrying out the President's program of reducing spending and increasing efficiency in Government.

Sawyer implemented a number of managerial changes, including restoring the documents sales program to a positive financial basis by reducing the inventory of unsalable publications, implementing a marketing program for Government documents, and creating a task force on documents pricing with the objective of increasing public access to lower-cost Government information while permitting GPO to recover all sales program costs. He also supported other modernization improvements, including upgrading press and binding equipment, and presided over the completion of the transition to electronic phototypesetting when the *Congressional Record* was completely converted from hot metal typesetting in January 1982. He supported a project of the Office of Management and Budget to identify excess printing capacity in Federal agencies, with the objective of increasing the amount of printing processed by GPO for procurement from the private sector.

Danford L. Sawyer, Jr., appointed by President Reagan, began his stormy tenure in 1981.

Sawyer's cost-cutting measures, however, led him into a confrontation with the JCP, then headed by Senator Charles McC. Mathias of Maryland, that ultimately tested the limits of the Public Printer's authority as a Presidential appointee under the policy direction of the JCP as GPO's board of directors. In early 1982, Sawyer proposed closing GPO's 24 bookstores nationwide, stating that the stores were losing money and that because the sales program operated predominately by mail order it would retain rather than lose the bookstore business. The JCP opted instead to refer the proposal to the General Accounting Office for review. The GAO's study was completed in 1983, with the finding that the bookstores were profitable. By then the closure proposal had been abandoned.

In March 1982, Sawyer announced a plan to furlough GPO employees one day every other week for six weeks to avert a projected financial loss in printing and binding operations. He contended he did not need the approval of the JCP to take this action and that he was not required to negotiate the matter with GPO's unions. In May 1982, the JCP adopted a resolution blocking the furlough pending further study. Sawyer announced the furloughs would proceed. The following month, 4,000

GPO employees held a "Truth March" down North Capitol Street to the west steps of the Capitol for a rally preceding a congressional hearing on the status of GPO's finances and the Public Printer's plans. Subsequently, ten unions belonging to GPO's Joint Council of Unions filed a writ of mandamus with the U.S. District Court for the District of Columbia seeking an order to compel the Public Printer to comply with the JCP resolution. In July 1982, the court handed down an opinion blocking the furlough plan based on the conclusion that the JCP was within its power in forbidding the furloughs pending further study. Assisted by the Justice Department, GPO filed an appeal before the U.S. Court of Appeals for the District of Columbia. In February 1983 the appeals court upheld the district court's decision. Meanwhile, the furlough plan was dropped when the projected financial losses did not materialize, but the damage in relations between Public Printer Sawyer and the JCP had been done.

The same applied to relations between Sawyer and GPO's unions. While they were able to cooperate on finalizing the first labor-management master agreement in GPO's history, covering all phases of work and working conditions, and also worked together to mount plaques honoring the veterans of World War II, the Korean Conflict, and the Vietnam Era in the GPO Veterans Landing in Building 1, they were unable to reach an agreement on wages. The wage dispute overlapped the furlough fight and turned increasingly bitter.

Between 1979 and 1982, management and labor had been unable to agree on wages at GPO, and the JCP had to make final settlements. In April 1982, Public Printer Sawyer's negotiating team proposed converting the GPO craft pay system to conform to pay rates established by the Federal wage board system, which was used to pay workers in other Federal printing facilities in the executive branch, and to end wage negotiations established by the Kiess Act. Management's proposal amounted to a 22% reduction in pay over the next three years. The proposal was submitted to a vote of union members and was rejected. Subsequently, the JCP appointed a factfinder to prepare a recommendation for a wage settlement. The fact finder recommended that Congress reject management's proposal and proposed a wage settlement. He found that

…GPO is not remotely comparable to any other Federal printing facility. As long as the GPO has as its primary task the

George Lord, Chairman, and Cornelius McIntyre, past chair of GPO's Joint Council of Unions, and GPO General Counsel Garrett Brown watch Public Printer Sawyer sign the first master labor agreement between GPO's unions and management. The single agreement covering all represented employees came after long and complex negotiations in 1982.

printing and publishing of the daily *Congressional Record* and the *Federal Register*...any attempt to equate its operations or its wage structure with that of other existing Federal printing facilities must be viewed as either ill-informed or unconcerned with the quality of GPO work and with its capacity to continue to furnish the service Congress has heretofore required of it.[32]

In September 1982 the JCP ordered a wage settlement based on the current pay system with annual cost of living adjustments. The following June, the GAO delivered a report on GPO's pay and classification system that had been requested by Congress. GAO found that GPO employees who collectively bargain received higher wages than did printing and lithographic employees at other Federal agencies or in private sector firms in the Washington, DC, area, and offered recommendations for new pay practices at GPO. However, the JCP dismissed the report because it failed to reference the work of the factfinder. A congressional hearing was held on the matter in late 1983 and legislation was introduced to change the GPO wage-setting system, but the bill was not passed. In the meantime, in various newspaper columns nationwide, a public relations campaign was conducted that sought to link the JCP with union campaign contributions, further contributing to the breakdown in relations between management and labor at GPO as well as between Sawyer and the JCP. In early 1984, Sawyer resigned office to return to the private sector.

A key development during the early 1980s that would have major implications for the future of GPO's relationship with Federal agencies in the executive branch was the Supreme Court's 1983 opinion in *INS* v. *Chadha*, invalidating the legislative veto. The Justice Department's Office of Legal Counsel deemed the JCP's powers over executive branch printing to be overruled by the decision.

In subsequent legal memoranda issued in 1984, the Department opined that the Department of Defense did not have to get the JCP's approval to establish its own printing facilities, and that the JCP's *Government Printing and Binding Regulations* were not binding on Federal agencies. For the moment the issue was primarily academic, but it was to resurface later in the decade as a serious challenge to GPO's printing authority.

Public Printer Kennickell and the End of Hot Metal Typesetting

After Public Printer Sawyer's resigned in early 1984, President Reagan nominated Ralph E. Kennickell, Jr., as Public Printer. A former Army officer who had served in Vietnam, Kennickell had worked for his family's printing company and had held other posts in the Reagan Administration. Following his nomination he received a recess appointment in December 1984. He subsequently was confirmed in December 1985, the youngest person ever appointed as Public Printer.

Public Printer Sawyer's plan to furlough the entire workforce roused the ire of employees and the Joint Committee on Printing alike. In June 1982 4,000 GPO employees marched down North Capitol Street to the Capitol for a rally.

*Ralph E. Kennickell, Jr.,
was the youngest person ever
appointed Public Printer.*

Kennickell restored labor-management relations with GPO's employees. Successful wage contract negotiations were concluded in 1985 that included a straight eight-hour day for craft employees (including a paid half-hour lunch period), implementation of double-pay for emergency work requirements such as inclement weather, and a payraise. In 1988, GPO employees represented by the American Federation of Government Employees (AFGE) were accorded wage bargaining rights by the JCP. GPO's unions began negotiations with management on implementing an alcohol- and drug-free workplace, which included workplace testing. Beyond labor/management relations, Kennickell reached out to GPO's employees in a number of ways large and small—including regular lunches with the Public Printer and GPO-wide events at local amusement parks—that echoed the efforts of Public Printer Carter. And like Carter, Kennickell broadened contacts with other national government printers around the globe, as well as with State government printers and the faculty of printing management colleges and universities.

It was Public Printer Kennickell who oversaw the end of hot metal typesetting at GPO in 1985, following the conversion of the *Congressional Record* to electronic text processing and phototypesetting systems in 1982. Nearly all of the Linotype and Monotype machines were removed from the building and sold off as scrap metal. Along with the General Pershing Linotype, GPO retained only two Linotypes for a limited amount of specialty typesetting, including setting titles for gold stamping in library binding. As Kennickell observed at the time,

> Composing has been the backbone of GPO's operation. In its heyday, the Composing Division comprised in excess of 150 Linotypes and Intertypes, 120 Monotype keyboards, and 125 casters, and in 1969 hit its high of 1,706 employees. A 1925 account reported that GPO had the capacity to machine-set the entire Bible within only six hours. The real story of hot metal composition at GPO is about the people who worked

there, experts not only in the craft of typesetting but of related fields as well. There were linguists, grammarians, and other experts to whom the Government turned time and again for the last word on language and usage. This versatility of the GPO compositor has always been reflected in the *GPO Style Manual*, an in-house product that is an industry standard. These were the skills that GPO turned to that ensured the successful development of its electronic printing system.

The decline of hot metal typesetting had an impact on GPO's building plans. By the early 1980s, with the failure to obtain congressional approval for a new facility at the Brentwood site, GPO was left with few options. In 1982, at the request of the JCP, the General Accounting Office performed a study of the need for a new building. The resulting report identified several alternatives that would lessen the problems caused by the physical characteristics of GPO's buildings, and urged cost/benefit analyses of these alternatives. Under Public Printer Sawyer, GPO performed the analyses and concluded it was less costly to remain in place, with a consolidation of operations in space that was freed up by the downsizing of composition functions. GPO began efforts

The last issue of the Congressional Record printed from stereotype plates struck from lead type, April 10, 1979. Hot metal typesetting ended altogether in 1985.

The GPO Style Manual

One of the most popular and widely-used documents produced by GPO is the *Government Printing Office Style Manual*, an official guide to the form and style of Federal Government printing. The Manual is issued under the authority of section 1105 of Title 44 of the United States Code, that requires the Public Printer to "determine the form and style in which the printing…ordered by a department is executed…having proper regard to economy, workmanship, and the purposes for which the work is executed." The *Manual* is prepared by the GPO Style Boad, composed of proofreading, printing, and Government documents specialists from within GPO.

The first *GPO Style Manual* appeared in 1894. It was developed primarily as a printers' stylebook to standardize word and type treatment and remains so today. Through successive editions, however, the *Manual* has come to be recognized by writers and editors both within and outside of the Federal Government as one of the most useful resources in the editorial arsenal. The 29th edition of the *Manual*, issued in 2000, formally introduced terms and usage for digital technology, and was the first *Manual* produced in CD-ROM and made available online. The 30th edition, released in 2008, was thoroughly redesigned to make it more modern and easier to read, the content was updated throughout, and incorporated many suggestions offered by users.

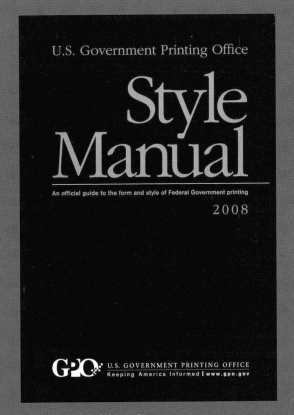

The 1908 GPO Style Manual

The 2008 GPO Style Manual

Joseph E. Jenifer receives his official appointment as Deputy Public Printer. When he became Acting Public Printer in 1988, he was the highest-ranking African-American official in GPO history.

to get out of leased facilities including the procurement and production functions located at the Navy Yard, and the library program operations located in Alexandria, VA, and move them back to North Capitol Street. The pattern of moving from leased to owned space characterized GPO's building plans for the remainder of the 20th century.

GPO continued to experience financial growth through the 1980s, with revenues climbing past $1 billion by 1989, the highest ever at that time. Under Public Printer Kennickell, regional procurement offices were expanded with the addition of six small satellite procurement offices serving special agency needs in San Antonio, Oklahoma City, Charleston, South Carolina, San Diego, Pittsburgh, and New Orleans, and printing procurement remained about at 75 percent of total revenues. The number of depository libraries grew to nearly 1,400, while the number of publications distributed to the libraries increased by more than one-third. GPO was responsible for a number of high profile publications during the decade, including the *Final Report of the President's Commission on the Challenger Space Shuttle Accident*, the *Iran-Contra Report*, and the *Report of the Attorney General's Commission on Pornography*.

But other signs emerged that GPO's conventional printing and distribution business had begun to decline, including reduced volumes of congressional work and postal card production. The amount of paper issued to production fell by about 10 percent. There were four fewer bookstores by the end of the 1980s, and the number of bookstore customers declined by more than a one-fourth by 1989 as did the overall number of publications sold by the sales program. Overall employment fell to 5,080 by 1989 as GPO continued to automate functions, especially in the composition area.

The Rise of Electronic Information Services and Products

The change in GPO's business was the result of the growing use of electronic information technologies government-wide, which by the mid-1980s was readily evident. GPO responded by beginning to offer electronic products and services such as CD–ROMs: in 1989, for example, a requisition for the procurement of the Defense Logistics Agency's Federal Logistics Data on CD–ROM resulted in the largest single procurement by GPO of this technology to that time. GPO also expanded "dialup" composition services linking its systems with remote computer-

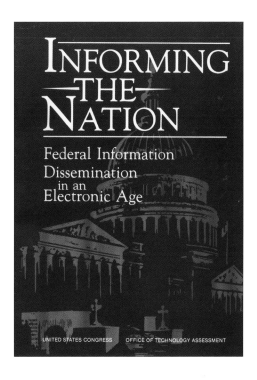

ized input in congressional and agency offices, established an electronic bulletin board for posting printing procurement bid information, and experimented with FM sideband dissemination and online dissemination. In 1984, GPO requested appropriations for the development of a Federal database of information but the request was rejected.

Later in the decade, GPO participated in a study of Federal information technology by the Office of Technology Assessment (OTA). OTA's widely read report, *Informing the Nation* (1987), found that the use of electronic information technologies "has outpaced the major Government-wide statutes that apply to Federal information dissemination," and recommended a redefining of "GPO's role in the dissemination of electronic formats," particularly to depository libraries, and "GPO's roles relative to the growth in agency desktop and high-end electronic publishing systems." GPO subsequently used the report to support efforts to expand its electronic information operations, which initially drew opposition from the Office of Management and Budget and elements of the private sector information industry.[33]

During this period, GPO and the Joint Committee on Printing, with the support of the library community and GPO's unions, worked to establish GPO's role in the emerging electronic era. Following the unsuccessful effort to reform Title 44 in the late 1970s, the JCP authorized GPO to sell electronic files and databases used in the printing process as Government publications, rather than as printed products, as GPO had been doing for several years. The JCP also took the position that publications on CD–ROMs were Government publications subject to the requirements of Title 44, and urged GPO to expand its efforts to provide electronic solutions for congressional and agency publications in response to growing demand throughout the Government. GPO and the JCP shared the view that GPO's statutory responsibilities for the production and dissemination of Government publications applied to publications in electronic as well as print formats. This view was later expressed in a 1990 opinion of GPO's General Counsel that "Congress did not intend to carve a distinction based upon the technology employed to disseminate Government publications. ..."

However, these views were not shared by all elements of the Government information community. Companies specializing in the electronic reproduction of Government information and publications argued that the private sector could provide these services more efficiently than Government, and that Government investment in electronic information services amounted to unfair competition. Supporters of Government provision of electronic information services argued that information dissemination was an inherent governmental function and that use of new and emerging technologies to promote broad and equitable public access to Government information access was part of that function.

This issue played itself out throughout the 1980s and into the early 1990s in debates between GPO, the JCP, and the library community, on the one hand, and the Office of Management and Budget under the Reagan and Bush Administrations on the other, on such matters as the revision of the OMB circular on Federal information dissemination and the revision of the Paperwork Reduction Act. The disadvantage GPO faced was the printing-focused language of Title 44 and the absence of a specific authority to provide electronic information products, such as tangible products like CD–ROMs and online services. Also problematic was how the provision of electronic information products and services, in an information environment that was increasingly decentralized as the result of electronic technology, could be reconciled with the statutory mandate to use GPO for print services. By the end of the decade, a scenario suggested by the Office of Technology Assessment—retaining the mandate to use GPO for print, and authorizing GPO to provide electronic services on a non-mandatory basis—seemed to offer a solution.

In the summer of 1989, Representative Jim Bates of California led hearings based on the OTA report. The hearings resulted, in early 1990, in the introduction of legislation to reform Title 44. GPO testified in support of the legislation that, among other things, would clarify its authority to produce and procure electronic formats, redefine "publication" to include electronic formats, expand the purpose of indexing to include publications in electronic formats, and set up a system for providing electronic information services to depository libraries. However, the bill was not reported out of committee and the effort to change Title 44 was abandoned.

While the debate over GPO's future was going on, the impact of the *Chadha* decision was revealed in 1987, when the Federal Acquisition Regulation (FAR) Council—composed of the Defense Department, the General Services Administration, and the National Aeronautics and Space Administration—published a notice in the *Federal Register* proposing to amend the FAR—the rules under which executive branch agencies purchase goods and services—to allow them to buy their own printing instead of using GPO as required by law. The proposal cited the *Chadha* decision and the Justice Department's opinions. Congress reacted by prohibiting the implementation of the FAR revision in a series of annual appropriations bills, upholding the principles and economies of centralized print production found in Title 44. The proposed revision was subsequently withdrawn quietly but the separation of powers issue it raised would be revisited again in the coming years.

After three years, Kennickell resigned to return to the private sector, leaving GPO under the direction of Acting Public Printer Joseph E. Jenifer, a career GPO employee who began his service as a temporary worker in GPO's printing plant in 1954. Jenifer graduated in 1961 from GPO's five-year apprenticeship program as a journeyman linotype operator and later joined GPO's newly created Electronic Photocomposition Section, working his way up through the ranks to become Deputy Public Printer in 1985. He was the first African-American employee ever appointed to GPO's second-highest office, and following Public Printer Kennickell's resignation in late 1988, he became the highest ranking African-American employee in GPO history, serving in that position until his retirement in March 1990. During the time he was in office, Jenifer testified on the impact of electronic information technologies, clearly indicating that GPO understood the challenges of the coming digital era. ❧

1991–2011

GPO IN THE DIGITAL ERA

A fundamental product of GPO's transition to electronic typesetting was the creation of electronic databases used for typesetting purposes. With the rise of electronic information technologies, those databases could be converted for online access by those seeking Government information. GPO's transition to electronic typesetting, begun in the 1960s and completed in the 1980s, thus set the stage for passage of the GPO Electronic Information Access Enhancement Act of 1993, the most important change to Title 44 since the Depository Library Act of 1962 and arguably since the 1895 Printing Act itself. Now empowered by statute to provide online access to the *Congressional Record*, the *Federal Register*, and other publications from all three branches of the Government, GPO created *GPO Access*, its first online information service, which appeared in 1994 just as Government and public use of the World Wide Web exploded. GPO's creative use of this service, including its policy for permanent public access to Government information, was critically important in fending off a wave of institutional challenges during the 1990s from a Congress and a White House determined to alter to role of conventional printing and distribution within Federal information policy.

As public use of digital Government information services increased in the first decade of the 21st century, some of those conventional services began to diminish, especially GPO's retail publications sales program, while others were combined with digital capabilities to create new product lines. Most prominently among the new products was the e-passport (an electronically-enhanced version of the traditional passport), that in the wake of the attacks of September 11, 2001, became an urgent requirement. Rapid change in information technologies also created an opportunity to re-engineer GPO's online offerings with the creation of a content management system to acquire, store, organize, and provide search and retrieval for the full range of digital documents. As GPO approached its 150th anniversary, its mission remained intact but its transformation into a digital information facility was well underway.

Public Printer Houk

President George H. W. Bush nominated Robert W. Houk as Public Printer. Houk had spent his career in the business forms printing industry. He was confirmed in March 1990. During his term, GPO issued *GPO/2001: Vision for New Millennium*, a strategic plan for GPO that embraced the use of electronic information technologies while improving the provision of conventional printing and distribution services, including the use of 100% recycled paper for regular use. Houk testified in support of early legislation to provide GPO with electronic dissemination authority.

Robert W. Houk was appointed by President George H.W. Bush in 1990.

PRESIDENT BUSH'S STATE OF THE UNION MESSAGE

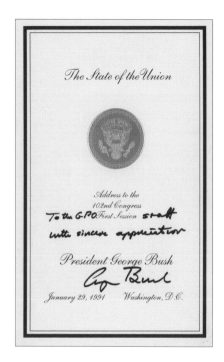

During Public Printer Houk's term, GPO received a copy of the State of the Union message personally inscribed by President George H. W. Bush "to the GPO staff with sincere appreciation." GPO had printed and delivered copies of the address in an exceptionally short timeframe. At 5:20 p.m. on January 29, 1991, the evening of the address, manuscript copy and a computer disk were delivered to GPO by the White House. The requirements were for 2,500 copies of an eight-page pamphlet with a gold-embossed cover, to be typeset, printed, bound, and delivered in three hours. In GPO's Electronic Photocomposition Division, the computer disk was first converted from one computer language to another. Composition was completed using GPO's Microcomp software, with output to a laser imagesetter. The imagesetter output was used for proofreading, correcting, and final page makeup. The Press Division photographed the camera-ready copy and produced and imposed the negatives. Offset plates were produced and the speech was printed on one of GPO's sheet-fed presses. The job then moved to the Binding Division where cutting, folding, inserting, stitching, trimming, and packaging were performed. The initial 1,200 copies left GPO for the Capitol with a DC Metropolitan Police escort at 7:50 p.m. The remaining copies were delivered at 8:20 p.m. That evening, Americans who watched President Bush deliver his State of the Union Address on television at 9 p.m. saw copies of the Address in the hands of those seated in the audience of the House chamber, a testimony to the dedication and expertise of GPO's skilled workforce.

Houk was immediately confronted by a highly critical report on GPO issued by the General Accounting Office (GAO). Entitled *Government Printing Office: Monopoly-Like Status Contributes to Inefficiency and Ineffectiveness*, the report's five principal findings said that GPO's operations were characterized by "costly, sometimes wasteful in-house production that relies on outdated equipment and does not focus on efficiency or quality; a procurement system that lacks necessary and readily available performance information and continues to award contracts to poorly performing contractors; poor communications with customers and poor systems for tracking and resolving customer complaints." It included seven recommendations for improvements and a suggestion that GPO should convene a group to explore GPO's "future role and mission".[34]

Although he did not agree with GAO's reference to GPO's "monopoly-like" status, Houk said he would use the report's recommendations as the basis for improvements. He intended to reduce costs, improve responsiveness to customers, modernize the plant and workforce, establish effective management performance plans, and determine GPO's future role in the Government. GPO developed an action plan to address GAO's recommendations and in October 1993 GAO told GPO the requirements of the report were fulfilled and no further action was necessary. The "monopoly" characterization, however, by that time had been adopted by Vice President Al Gore's Reinventing Government initiative as a rationale for proposals to decentralize Government printing, and would be raised again over the next several years.

Public Printer DiMario

Michael F. DiMario became President Clinton's appointee in 1993.

After Houk resigned office in early 1993, President Bill Clinton appointed Michael F. DiMario as Public Printer. A former Air Force intelligence officer and an attorney by training, DiMario was a long-time GPO official who had held virtually every senior management appointment in the agency, including Deputy General Counsel, Superintendent of Documents, and Administrative Law Judge as well as key positions at the head of the Printing Procurement Department and Production operations. During his term, he oversaw the establishment and growth of *GPO Access* and the transition of the depository library program to a predominantly electronic basis, implemented computer-to-plate and other electronic improvements including online bid solicitations, guided GPO in preparing its computer systems for the possible effects of the changeover to the Year 2000, supported environmental reforms, and continued the reduction of staffing levels and other costs. DiMario faced some of the most direct challenges to GPO from Congress and the executive branch, and during a time of technology transition it fell to him to implement the new *GPO Access* law while articulating the continuing role of printing in Federal information policy. Including his service as Acting Public Printer prior to his appointment by the President, DiMario's term at GPO's helm from 1993–2002 was the third longest in the agency's history, after Public Printers Giegengack and Carter.

Passage of the GPO Access Act

Congressional efforts in the late 1970s and the late 1980s to address the growth of electronic alternatives to the conventional Government printing and distribution system through comprehensive reform of Title 44 had been unsuccessful. In 1991, a new effort was undertaken, supported by the depository library community and public interest groups, to give GPO specific authority to provide electronic information services. Public Printer Houk supported this concept in hearings in 1991, as did Public

Printer DiMario in 1993. The effort culminated that year with the passage of the GPO Electronic Information Access Enhancement Act, directing GPO to establish a system of online access to the *Congressional Record* and the *Federal Register* and such other publications as determined by the Superintendent of Documents, an electronic storage facility, and a Federal information locator. The system was to be developed using funds from savings in the reduction of the distribution of printed information. GPO was to provide online access free of charge to depositories and was authorized to charge others for the service.

This landmark legislation gave GPO the necessary authority to assume an essential role in the provision of information services and ended a decade-long argument over GPO's involvement in electronic information dissemination. GPO was required to have the system operating in one year. Service was begun in June 1994 as *GPO Access*. With the system, GPO adopted a unique policy of providing permanent public access to information posted online, based on the system of permanent access

Satellite trucks of the news media gather outside Building 1 for the annual release of the President's budget.

President Clinton signed the GPO Access act (P.L. 103-40) in 1993.

provided through GPO's partnership with regional depository libraries. *GPO Access* won multiple awards throughout the 1990s. By the end of the decade, GPO's provision of Government documents in both print and electronic formats—including the annual Federal budget, the documents associated with the impeachment of President Clinton, the judicial decisions in the celebrated Microsoft case, and others—had become the accustomed norm. GPO initially developed a system of subscriptions to *GPO Access* as authorized by law, but there were relatively few subscribers and in 1995 Public Printer DiMario ordered an end to the practice of charging users. Thereafter, use of the service grew exponentially. By the end of the decade *GPO Access* offered more than 225,000 titles and was providing 228,000,000 document retrievals annually. Meanwhile, system development and operating costs fell far under the original cost estimates from the Congressional Budget Office.

"Reinventing Government" and the "Contract with America"

The enactment of electronic authority for GPO was timely, as the White House and Congress began to take up a series of proposals to alter the role of conventional printing and distribution within Federal information policy. Some of these proposals emerged within the framework of the separation of powers, echoing similar arguments advanced during the Wilson and Truman administrations, and were given new life by the 1983 *Chadha* decision. Others were raised within the context of private/public sector provision of printing and information services, a longstanding issue that had been tempered by GPO's partnership with the printing industry under the printing procurement program. The emergence of these issues signaled an intent by both Congress and the White House to move Government printing and information policy in the direction of digital technology and their willingness to consider fundamental institutional change for GPO in order to achieve that goal.

In 1993, under the leadership of Vice President Gore, the Clinton Administration released its recommendations for "reinventing Government," an effort to create a Government that "works better and costs less."[35] Included in this initiative was the claim that GPO was a "monopoly," along with proposals to end congressional control over executive branch printing and make GPO compete with other Government agencies and the private sector for printing contracts.

Computer tape library, Data Systems Division.

THE STARR REPORT

In the late summer and fall of 1998, GPO printed one of the highest profile Government documents of the decade, the report of the Independent Counsel on the investigation of President Clinton, the Starr Report, formerly titled *Communication from Kenneth W. Starr, Independent Counsel, Transmitting a Referral to the United States House of Representatives Filed in Conformity with the Requirements of Title 28, United States Code, Section 595c*. The report, with accompanying appendices totaled more than 8,000 pages, and all were produced under short time frames and high security conditions established by the House Judiciary Committee. The materials were also posted on *GPO Access*. The report was used in the impeachment of the President in late 1998 and his subsequent trial in early 1999 by the Senate, that acquitted him. The printing and online dissemination of these documents drew attention and praise from the *Wall Street Journal* for GPO's "Herculean labors."

The Administration also recommended that information distribution to depository libraries be performed instead by the agencies, and that other GPO distribution functions be similarly restructured in the executive branch.

Public Printer DiMario testified before Congress that the decentralization of Government printing among agencies would increase costs, reduce competitiveness in Government print procurement, and reduce public access to Government information. While recognizing the usefulness of electronic information dissemination and GPO's role in providing electronic public access, he also provided a clear statement on the continuing utility of printing in Government information policy:

> Ink-on-paper today is still the most egalitarian of information formats. It is accessible, transportable, and economical. The increased dissemination of Government information in electronic formats should indeed be pursued. ...But at this time electronic technologies must be utilized in addition to, not in place of, proven systems of Government information reproduction and dissemination, and protections must be provided for those who do not have access to computers and the other technologies necessary to make electronic access meaning-

ful. For if we are not careful about maintaining policies to provide for the efficient and equitable access of all citizens to Government information, we run the risk of turning into a Nation of information-haves and information have-nots: a Nation of information elites, equipped with technology, and a Nation of the information-dispossessed, shut out by technology from access to critical information by and about Government that is essential to life in the United States today.

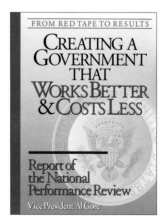

The concerns raised by GPO and others were enough to lead to the tabling of the legislation proposed by the Administration in 1994, but the concept of decentralizing Government printing by transferring GPO's functions elsewhere would reappear later.

The 1994 congressional elections brought new leadership to Congress that sought to implement its "Contract with America" by changing a Government that was "too big and spends too much."

Terminal for the Atex photocomposition system, Electronic Photocomposition Division.

Disk drives, Electronic Photocomposition Division.

Among other issues, the 104th Congress took up proposals that sought to privatize Government printing and reduce the scope of GPO and its operations. None of the introduced versions advanced beyond hearings and, although a comprehensive printing reform bill was introduced in the final days of the 104th Congress, there were no hearings. A common feature of these bills was the proposal to abolish the Joint Committee on Printing, which eventually was taken up by Congress. Subsequent legislative branch appropriations acts reduced the JCP's funding and then eliminated it beginning with the 106th Congress. The Committee's authority was not abolished, however, but was exercised thereafter by staff of the House Administration and Senate Rules and Administration Committees on an *ad hoc* basis.

The opportunity to generate savings from *GPO Access* was taken up quickly by the new congressional leadership, which required GPO to study the transition to a more electronic Federal Depository Library Program. The *Study to Identify Measures Necessary for a Successful Transition to a More Electronic Federal Depository Library Program* was published in June 1996. The rapid transition period of two years originally proposed by the study raised concerns in the library community, which in 1996 reported only 38% of depositories could offer the public even one up-to-the-minute personal computer with Web browser software and full Internet connection. The community advised that a transition plan of five to seven years would be more practical, and that period was implemented. Thereafter, savings generated by printing less for distribution to depository libraries were used to help fund *GPO Access*.

Relations with the Executive Branch

During the Clinton Administration, the dispute between Congress and the executive branch over control of Government printing came to a head. Although this was a longstanding point of contention dating to the Wilson and Truman administrations, the dispute had its immediate origins in 1991, when Congress enacted a permanent bar on the 1987 attempt to revise the Federal Acquisition Regulations—which would have allowed given agencies their own printing authority—by requiring all printing to be performed by GPO. The following year, the prohibition was amended to apply to all executive branch printing paid for by appropriations. The General Services Administration, which was authorized to

GPO produced and distributed CD–Rom versions of many popular publications throughout the 1990s.

provide in-house printing services to regional Federal agencies, sought a Justice Department opinion on the constitutionality of this provision. The Department responded in 1993 that it was permissible because "it does not give the GPO the authority to refuse to print any materials, but merely requires that printing be procured by or through GPO."

A year later, Congress amended the 1992 provision to include "duplicating" within the definition of printing. President Clinton signed it into law, but said the provision raised "serious constitutional concerns," and between 1994 and 1996 there were multiple efforts by the Office of Management and Budget and Congress to work out a compromise position. These efforts collapsed in May 1996, when the Department of Justice issued an opinion finding that the extent of congressional control over executive branch printing violated the separation of powers and was

Computer-to-plate processing, Digital Prepress Division.

126

unconstitutional. The 1996 opinion also said that executive branch officials would not be held liable for ordering printing in violation of the law, irrespective of the opposite view held by the General Accounting Office. One observer remarked that this development reflected a "serious deterioration of interbranch comity."[36]

In response to these developments, Senator John Warner of Virginia, Chairman of the Joint Committee on Printing, led an effort with Senator Wendell Ford of Kentucky to develop a comprehensive reform bill. Hearings were held in 1997, and in 1998 a bill was introduced containing sweeping revisions to Title 44 aimed at addressing the separation of powers issue and modernizing the statute to provide GPO with more effective authorities in an increasingly electronic era. The bill received broad support from Public Printer DiMario, the library community, labor, public interest groups, and other stakeholders but fell short of the backing it needed in Congress to ensure passage. Though reported to the Senate floor late in the closing days of the 105th Congress, it was not passed before Congress adjourned.

Service Improvements and Financial Cutbacks

Against the backdrop of Administration and congressional proposals to reform GPO were a number of key changes in GPO's operations. In 1995 GPO installed three new 64-page web offset presses to replace the four letterpresses originally installed in 1953 and 1973 to print the *Congressional Record* and the *Federal Register*. In 1998, GPO introduced state-of-the-art computer-to-plate technology, generating significant cost savings. Fiber optic links with Congress were expanded for remote access to GPO's composition system, increasing the volume of congressional copy received electronically. The relocation of the Office of the Federal Register across H Street NW from GPO facilitated the installation of a laser link for the transmission of publishing data. As the new century approached, GPO joined with the rest of Government, industry, and technology professionals to prepare its computerized business and production systems for the possible problems for computers at the beginning of year 2000, known as Y2K.

The 1990s also saw the implementation of key environmental improvements for recycled paper and vegetable oil-based inks. GPO's initial use of 100% recycled newsprint for the *Congressional Record* and

the *Federal Register* ran from 1991 to 1997, when the company producing it ceased production; thereafter, recycled newsprint contracts were for paper with the minimum 40% postconsumer waste content until 2009. In 1993, legislation was introduced to require the use of vegetable oil-based inks in Government printing to reduce dependence on foreign oil, rely on a domestically produced resource, and result in an environment-friendly product. GPO supported the legislation and it was enacted in 1994. Since then, with the exception of security inks, all inks used by GPO for in-house and procured printing meet the statutory standard for including vegetable oil-based inks, made primarily from soybean oil.

At the same time, GPO's financial position was eroding due to an abrupt decline in printing demand in the early 1990s, primarily from the Department of Defense. As public use of *GPO Access* and other Federal Web services expanded, those who formerly relied on the publications from GPO's sales program turned increasingly to free Web access, resulting in financial losses as revenue from the sale of publications fell by more than one-third. Public Printer DiMario responded to the reduced business volume by securing wage concessions affecting work hours and nightwork pay, consolidating operations from leased to owned space, and reducing the workforce through retirement incentives and attrition to a decade-long total of more than 35%. By the end of the 1990s GPO employed fewer workers than at any other time in the 20th century.

These and other measures were outpaced by falling revenues, however, and by 1999 GPO had sustained more than $30 million in operating losses throughout the decade, to which were added an additional $17 million in losses from other reporting requirements. GPO used money in its revolving fund that was set aside for investment in new plant and equipment to absorb the losses and did not ask Congress for supplemental appropriations. It continued to receive favorable audit opinions throughout this period, as it had historically. An exhaustive management study of GPO by Booz-Allen & Hamilton, Inc., requested by the House Appropriations Committee late in the decade, reported broad support for GPO's plant production, printing procurement, and documents dissemination programs across the Government, a finding that stood in marked contrast to the GAO report issued at the beginning of the 1990s. Nevertheless, by decade's end GPO's financial resources were significantly depleted.

A New Logo for GPO

In 2003, GPO unveiled a new logo to take the place of the 1907 logo that had been reintroduced by Public Printer Kennickell in 1985. The new logo was adopted by GPO "to symbolize its transformation from an ink-on-paper provider to a digital data delivery organization. The new logo reflects GPO's determination to meet the evolving information needs of its client agencies and to serve an increasingly digital-aware American public." The elements of the new logo were purposely selected to demonstrate the historical progression in printing. The "G" was modified from a traditional typeface, Times New Roman, which marked a change from type derived from handwritten text to more legible type forms used in a mechanical printing press. The "P" alluded to woodblock, hot metal, and Linotype technologies, reflecting a modern era in printing and publication in its sans serif typeface. The "O" was a digitally modified form of an oldstyle face, ITC Galliard, representing an integration of past, present, and future. Pixel shapes are incorporated to further suggest digital and electronic processes.

As part of the effort to reduce costs, GPO shed its regional printing plants in New York, San Francisco, Chicago, and at the Washington, DC, Navy Yard. The Chicago regional printing plant for many years was the producer of the *Commerce Business Daily*, the Government's compendium of contracting opportunities, which was supplanted by a Web site called *FedBizOps*. For a brief period in the 1990s GPO also took over the management of a field printing plant in Juneau, AK, formerly operated by the General Services Administration. During the 1990s, all were closed or, in the case of the Navy Yard facility, consolidated with the main GPO printing plant. The Denver operation, which was cleared for classified work, stayed open until 2003, when it was finally closed.

GPO's bookstores also were targeted for closure. During the 1990s, the number of publications sold annually fell from 28.5 million to 8.9 million, and by 2001 the number was down to less than seven million. To offset the loss of business, GPO cut sales staffing, reduced its inventory, increased prices on the remaining items, and offered improvements including a secure Web-based ordering service and expanded credit card payment acceptance. Along with these actions, GPO began closing bookstores in 2001. Bookstores in San Francisco, McPherson Square in Washington, DC, Boston, and Philadelphia were closed that year, and the stores in Chicago, Cleveland, Columbus, and Birmingham followed in 2002.

GPO Enters the 21st Century

The GPO that closed out the 1990s—and the twentieth century—was smaller, less industrialized, and computerized far beyond the imagination of anyone in the "big shop" that began the century. But it remained intact and prepared to face the challenges of the future.

No one could have envisioned the first of those challenges, however, as GPO—like everyone else in the Nation—watched the terrorist attacks of September 11, 2001, unfold in New York and Washington, DC. In the aftermath, GPO looked for ways it could help. A secure area was set up on GPO's Web site so that employees of the Equal Employment Opportunity Commission's regional office, which had been destroyed at the World Trade Center complex, could continue working from home. Personnel from GPO's Inspector General's office assisted with rescue and recovery efforts in New York and at the Pentagon. Later that autumn, when mailed packages containing anthrax forced the closure of House and Senate office buildings, GPO provided space for personnel from the Office of the Clerk of the House and the Senate Legislative Counsel, and turned over its loading docks in Building 4 to the Capitol Police for use in screening deliveries to Capitol Hill. GPO also set up an emergency printing facility at its Laurel, MD, warehouse, and stepped up security procedures at its main offices, including the installation of magnetometers and other screening equipment at building entrances.

In the wake of 9/11, Federal agencies began reviewing their information products for security issues. The U.S. Geological Survey asked GPO to withdraw from depository libraries and destroy copies of a CD–ROM entitled *Source Area Characteristics of Large Public Surface-Water Supplies in the Coterminous United States: An Information Resource for Source-Water Assessment*. Unlike other withdrawal requests typically involving superseded or outdated information, this was a request to withdraw information based on sensitivity determined by other events. The process led GPO to revise its document withdrawal guidelines to fully involve the requesting agency and the library community in future document withdrawals.

The institutional challenges to GPO of the 1990s were renewed early in the administration of President George W. Bush, when the Office of Management and Budget issued a new separation of powers challenge to GPO's printing authority. OMB Memorandum M–02–07, "Printing and Duplicating Through the Government Printing Office" (May 2002), echoed the Justice Department's opinions on the *Chadha* decision, the 1987 FAR revision proposal, and the Clinton Administration's reinventing Government initiative by instructing the heads of executive departments and agencies to produce or procure their printing work wherever they wished, without regard to the requirement in Title 44 to use GPO. In hearings before Congress that summer, Public Printer DiMario testified that OMB's proposal would potentially increase Federal printing costs significantly, in addition to limiting public access to Government information. OMB announced it would procure the printing of the *Budget of the U.S. Government* itself, instead of producing it through GPO as it had done previously. In response, Congress included language in a continuing appropriations resolution later that year blocking OMB from producing the *Budget* other than at GPO. GPO, for its part, revised its cost estimate for the publication to offer OMB a savings over the previous year's cost. OMB accepted the new estimate and pledged to work through GPO. Its proposal on executive printing remained pending, however.

Public Printer James

In the midst of this controversy, President Bush nominated Bruce R. James as Public Printer. A graduate of Rochester Institute of Technology's School of Printing Management and Sciences, James had spent his career in the print and information industry where he developed several companies,

including a law publishing company. He was confirmed by the Senate in November 2002. "Throughout my life I have used technology to enhance the ability to get information into the hands of people, and this was a task I was up to taking on," James said. Promising to uphold the printing laws until Congress changed them, James proposed to resolve the dispute with OMB by creating a printing "compact" that would provide agencies with more choice and potentially reduce costs while keeping printing within the requirements of the law. In June 2003, OMB and GPO jointly announced this agreement, and OMB's directive was quietly withdrawn.

President George W. Bush appointed Bruce R. James in 2002.

GPO's nationwide contract with Kinkos (later FedEx Office), known as GPO *Express*™, initially awarded in 2005, was the printing procurement solution that included several of the compact's characteristics. The contract covered the production of quick-turnaround printing that previously had been provided through multiple regionally located commercial printers. The new convenience printing contract offered a standardized package of service capabilities via a pricing schedule that provided significant discounts off of the vendor's regular prices. The objective was to capture printing and duplicating that previously had escaped from GPO's procurement and dissemination system, resulting in higher costs to agencies and instances of eligible documents not being distributed to depositories. Along with this contract, GPO increased the dollar limit on simplified purchase agreements, expanding the ability of agencies to procure products and services directly from lists of prequalified vendors without first going through GPO.

In December 2004, GPO published its *Strategic Vision for the 21st Century*, the result of a planning initiative that had commenced on James' arrival, and based in part on a GAO review of GPO begun earlier during the controversy with OMB. The document articulated the impact of digital technology on GPO:

> Throughout its history, GPO has been organized to carry
> out its mission in a traditional printing craft setting with its

SMART CARDS

The success of GPO's conversion to e-passports and the emergence of the need for other secure credentials in the post-9/11 period provided an opportunity for a new product line for GPO. In 2007, the agency established a capability for the production of secure Federal credentials, known as smart cards, in Building 3. These included the production of secure credentials for law enforcement personnel involved with the 2009 Presidential inauguration; hundreds of thousands of cards for the

Department of Homeland Security's Customs and Border Protection, such as the Trusted Traveler Program cards NEXUS, SENTRI, and FAST cards, which give pre-approved travelers faster service in crossing America's northern and southern borders; as well as cards for Medicaid recipients in Puerto Rico, Federal Inspectors General, and other identification programs. In 2010, GPO's smart card production facility was certified by the General Services Administration as the only Government facility capable of providing Federal agency identification cards meeting the standards of Homeland Security Presidential Directive (HSPD)–12, issued in 2006.

emphasis on extensive capital investments in heavy metal equipment operated in a large factory environment. While GPO's mission will remain essentially the same in the future, the introduction of digital technology has changed the ways its products and services will be created and how they will look and function to meet the ever-changing needs of the Federal Government and the way public users of Government information now prefer it. …Therein lies the biggest challenge for the Government Printing Office.

The key initiatives established by the *Vision* were projects to develop a flexible digital information content system for Federal documents; leverage the value of GPO's aging buildings against the cost of building a new printing and digital information factory; expand the production of security and intelligent documents, including passports and other documents; reorganize GPO around business lines or units; import digital solutions to GPO's ongoing business needs; and expand training opportunities for employees. These objectives were to guide GPO operations for the remainder of the decade.

The development of a new digital content system was the primary outcome of the *Strategic Vision* document. By the early 2000s, the limitations of *GPO Access* had become readily apparent. The system relied on a dated search and retrieval system called WAIS (Wide Area Information System) with limited capabilities, a fact acknowledged in GPO's appropriations requests for fiscal years 2003 and 2004, when funds were requested to upgrade the system. *GPO Access* was also unable to function as a platform for other digital ingest, storage, production, and dissemination capabilities proposed by the *Strategic Vision*.

The purpose of the new digital content system, named the Federal Digital System, or FDsys, was to "organize, manage, and output authenticated content for any use or purpose and to preserve the content independent of specific hardware or software so that it can be migrated forward and preserved for the benefit of future generations." It would be designed to house "all known Federal Government documents within the scope of the Federal Depository Library Program, whether printed or born digital." These would be "cataloged and authenticated and then entered into a system according to GPO metadata and document creation

standards," to be available later for "Web searching and Internet viewing, downloading and printing, and as document masters for conventional and on-demand printing, or other digital requirements." The system was to be developed in three stages, or releases, with Release 1 equivalent to a replacement of *GPO Access* with new search and retrieval capabilities and other enhancements. Release 1 of FDsys went live in early 2009, to positive reviews from the press and public. Once all of the databases were migrated and upgraded from *GPO Access* to FDsys, *GPO Access* was slated for shut down.

With the release *GPO Access* in 1994, GPO had begun providing online access to the *Congressional Record*, the *Federal Register*, and other congressional and agency publications. No provision was made in GPO's online authorization for providing access to documents issued before that date. To remedy that situation, GPO's *Strategic Vision* proposed digitizing all Federal publications issued prior to 1994 for inclusion in this system. In 2010, GPO developed a proposal to work collaboratively

Public Printer James greets President Bush during the presentation of the first volume of the President's Public Papers in 2003.

with the Library of Congress to digitize the 1951–2002 volumes of the Statutes at Large as well as all volumes of the *Congressional Record*, in addition to other core legislative, legal, and regulatory documents to be named later. The project was approved by the JCP, marking a significant new line of work for GPO in carrying out its mission to keep America informed.

Another key objective of the *Strategic Vision* was a plan to offer GPO's buildings and property to a commercial developer in exchange for the construction of a new, modern printing and digital production facility. Public Printer James argued that GPO's buildings were aging, costly to maintain, and too large for GPO's future needs. In addition to obtaining a new facility, the lease of the main structure, comprising GPO Buildings 1–3, would generate income that could be used for investment in plant and

Work on the official portrait of President Obama, 2009.

equipment, which in turn would decrease GPO's needs for future appropriations. GPO proposed to sell Building 4 outright to raise the funds to finance the move and help furnish and equip the new facility.

In 2005, GPO contracted with the Staubach Company to develop its building proposal and design a new facility. The plan would require a change to GPO's financial authority under Title 44 to allow GPO to lease property and retain the proceeds without returning them to the Treasury. The plan was generally well received on Capitol Hill, as long as Congress was permitted right of first refusal for vacated space at GPO, the new GPO was located within the Washington, DC, city limits, and the plan did not impose a significant financial burden on appropriations. This last condition proved to be too difficult to surmount. A draft bill developed by the Senate Rules and Administration Committee was "scored" by the Congressional Budget Office with a potential impact on appropriations of between $300 and $400 million, causing the relocation plan to be set aside.

Restoring GPO's financial position was another objective of the *Strategic Vision*. In 2003, with an appropriation to the revolving fund of $10 million, GPO conducted an early retirement incentive program, or buyout, that reduced employment rolls by more than 300 positions for a savings of an estimated $21.7 million annually. All the remaining bookstores except the main store at GPO itself were closed. A second buyout was conducted in 2004, reducing employment another 250 positions for an additional annual savings of $18.1 million. The combined savings from these efforts in fiscal year 2004 resulted in a consolidated financial gain of $11.3 million, the first since fiscal year 1998. This financial result was followed by a succession of year-end gains in most years throughout the rest of the decade, providing funds for increased investment in new equipment and technology.

Public Printer Tapella

In April 2006, Public Printer James announced he would resign office to return to the private sector in January 2007. In May 2007, President Bush nominated Robert C. Tapella as Public Printer. He was confirmed in October. Before becoming Public Printer, Tapella had served as Deputy Chief of Staff and later Chief of Staff to James. He had more than a decade of experience as a professional staff member of the House of Representatives. He also had a background and degree in graphic communications from California Polytechnic State University in San Luis Obispo.

Robert C. Tapella was appointed Public Printer by President Bush in 2007.

An architect of GPO's *Strategic Vision*, Tapella took office committed to continuing the program begun under James. He pursued this through the development of FDsys, the ongoing replacement of GPO's legacy computer systems with an integrated suite of business systems, expanded digital services for Federal agencies, and the establishment of a backup facility for the production of e-passports. Tapella also made sustainable environmental stewardship an ongoing strategic initiative for GPO and continued to call for a new GPO building.

GPO's development of electronic or e-passports heralded a new generation of mixed digital and print products. In the late 1990s, the United States and other nations agreed to use an electronic chip in passports to standardize and enhance the operability of passports at borders around the world. The chips were to be compliant with a standard established by the International Civil Aviation Organization, a UN-based organization. After 9/11, the concept of the chips acquired an additional importance for establishing secure identification. In 2004, GPO solicited bids for the chip technology, including the chip itself and an antenna assembly, to be incorporated into the passport covers. No U.S.-based offerors came forward, and after a round of testing and evaluation involving GPO, the State Department, the National Institute of Standards and Technology, and other Federal agencies, contracts were awarded to two overseas chip manufacturers for the chip and antenna production and insertion into the passport covers. In the meantime, GPO developed and installed a new IT infrastructure in Building 4 to support the production and administration of e-passports and implemented additional protections to ensure the security of the passport production and delivery process, including delivery by armored carriers to replace GPO and commercial deliveries.

In 2006, after the installation of additional equipment and testing, GPO began producing e-passports, and by 2007 production of conventional print-only passports ended and e-passports became GPO's sole passport product line. This imposed additional administrative requirements

THE LONGEST-SERVING EMPLOYEES

In 1933, an extraordinary GPO employee reached the milestone of 60 years of service. He was W. Andrew (Andy) Smith (1854–1941), who came to work at GPO as a messenger in 1873 and spent the next 68 years at GPO, most of them as either Congressional Record Clerk or Assistant Clerk. Smith was described as "an efficient, faithful, devoted employee of GPO" who worked until the day before his death, at age 87, on May 14, 1941.

Five years later, Virginia F. Saunders joined GPO as a typist in the Public Documents Division, probably little imagining that she would very nearly equal Andy Smith's remarkable record of service. Smith had devoted his career to the *Congressional Record*. Saunders moved into her place of distinction in 1969, when Superintendent of Documents Carper W. Buckley singled her out to take over the compilation of the *Congressional Serial Set*. At first she demurred, saying "I don't know enough about congressional documents." Buckley persisted and eventually persuaded Saunders to take the job on a trial basis. Over the next 40 years, she became a recognized expert on the history and

function of the *Serial Set* and the recognized authority both within and outside GPO on its compilation and production. She had friends and admirers throughout GPO, the nationwide library community, and on Capitol Hill, not only because of her long service, but for her dedication and concern for the perpetuation and improvement of the *Serial Set*. She was recognized in 1989 by GPO and President George H.W. Bush for a modification to the makeup of the *Serial Set* that saved taxpayers an estimated $600,000 in the cost of including the Iran-Contra hearings. She served with distinction on a study group that substantially revised and modernized the makeup of the *Serial Set* in 1994. And four times Members of Congress rose to pay tribute to her in the *Congressional Record:* on her 50th and 60th anniversaries, when she received the James Bennett Childs Award from the Government Documents Roundtable of the American Library Association in 1999, and at the time of her death.

In early 2009, Virginia Saunders was interviewed by a *Washington Post* reporter for a feature about her long service. He asked her about retirement and she replied, "As long as my health is pretty good, I intend to hang in with my boots on." Despite failing health, she continued to serve in her position, and she died, with her boots still on, on June 19, 2009, after 63 years of service.

on GPO and the State Department, including developing accurate pricing and the financing of technology and equipment upgrades, all covered by a formal memorandum of understanding between the two agencies. GPO's production capabilities for the e-passport were challenged in 2007 and in 2008 when public demand for passports escalated sharply, largely in response to new identification requirements for travel in North America and the Caribbean. GPO's production of e-passports jumped to 23.5 million in FY 2008, compared with 19.3 million in fiscal year 2007 and 13.1 million in 2006. To meet the demand, GPO expanded production to two full shifts and authorized significant overtime, enabling it to meet scheduled requirements with no delay in delivery. By fiscal years 2009 and 2010, annual passport production subsided to 10.5 million and 13.2 million, respectively. In 2010, GPO issued a Request for Proposals (RFP) for a new chip assembly contract.

To support the State Department's need for a backup capability to produce passports, and with Joint Committee on Printing approval, GPO created a second passport production facility in 2008 in an unused

A second facility for passport production was opened in Stennis, Mississippi, in 2008.

complex at the Stennis Space Center in Mississippi. New press and bindery equipment was procured, 47 personnel were hired and trained (helping to provide additional employment in an area devastated by Hurricane Katrina in 2005), and secure IT and communications systems were established to support passport production five days per week, on one shift. This was the first remote production facility established by GPO in the post-World War II period. In 2010, both the Washington, DC, and Stennis passport production facilities achieved certification by the International Standards Organization (ISO) as complying with ISO 9001, signaling that GPO's passport production operations meet globally recognized standards of excellence for production and quality processes.

Public Printer Tapella made sustainable environmental stewardship a key initiative for GPO, building on GPO's conversion to recycled paper and vegetable oil-based inks in the 1990s, and arguing that it made good business sense:

> In the past, environmental issues for our industry were a matter of compliance with laws and regulations. But now we're looking ahead to the future. And the future is sustainable environmental stewardship, which is more than just going green: it is being proactive and making changes so that we are a more efficient operation. … Sustainable environmental stewardship is not a partisan issue. It's good business, and it's good government.

To carry out this initiative, GPO began developing plans to move from web offset presses to digital equipment to reduce paper consumption; accelerated the re-engineering of business processes to take advantage of the efficiencies of digital technology; conducted energy audits to reduce energy demand throughout GPO; evaluated paper that goes beyond the minimum standards for recycled content; reduced the waste generated by GPO's production processes; and installed "green" roofs on GPO's buildings that feature an energy-efficient, bio-based roofing system. In 2009, GPO increased the postconsumer waste content of the recycled newsprint used in the production of the *Congressional Record* and *Federal Register* to 100% from the previous level of 40% at no additional cost, earning the recognition of Speaker of the House of Representatives Nancy Pelosi. In other actions, the agency upgraded GPO's vehicle fleet with more fuel efficient and environmentally friendly vehicles using funds appropriated to the General Services Administration by the 2009 economic stimulus bill, and adopted technologies to reduce emissions and cut GPO's waste stream.[37]

Tapella also amended his predecessor's building plan to focus on development of a new structure on unimproved GPO property immediately west of the buildings, on land currently used for parking. A new structure would include space for House and Senate offices as well as GPO, while GPO's older buildings would be turned over for commercial development. However, a report on the plan issued by the GAO in early 2009 recommended a review of other building alternatives, and was unable to provide guidance on how to address the issue of the budget "score" that had hobbled the previous plan.[38]

Public Printers James and Tapella emphasized investment in new equipment as a means to develop and support new product lines for GPO. Along with the production of smart cards, these included presses for printing color documents in-house. A key use of an enhanced in-house color printing capability came in 2009, when GPO printed the official portraits of President Barack Obama and Vice President Joe Biden. Copies of the photos were distributed by the General Services Administration to more than 7,000 Federal facilities worldwide and made available by GPO for sale to the public.

Another example of expanded product offerings came when GPO's FDsys capabilities were used to support the Obama Administration's Open Government Initiative. In 2009, in cooperation with the Office of the *Federal Register*, GPO provided *Federal Register* data in extensible markup language (XML) format to a new Web site, data.gov. The following year, GPO assisted the Office of the Federal Register in the development of *Federal Register 2.0*, a state-of-the-art application for providing access to *Federal Register* information, featuring a new layout that organizes the content by topics, similar to the organization of a newspaper Web site.

The ongoing transition to accessing Government information electronically had a significant impact on GPO's Superintendent of Documents operations in the 2000s. In GPO's sales program, the number of publications sold dropped from 7.4 million in 2000 to 1.1 million by decade's end, reflecting the end of brick-and-mortal retail sales by 2003. Online sales began to grow, however, and with the modernization of the main bookstore in 2010 and the introduction of new products, including a partnership with Google for e-Books, the business seemed to have stabilized. The number of copies of tangible publications distributed to depository libraries continued to fall during the decade, from 12.2 million in 2000 to 3.2 million in 2009, and program operations continued to shift to an expanded range of electronic collection management responsibilities. By the end of the decade the number of depository libraries had declined to 1,239, and calls were growing for changes to the Depository Library Act to adapt it to current technology and the ways Government information can be made accessible to the public today.

Public Printer Boarman

In April 2010, President Obama nominated William J. Boarman as Public Printer. Boarman had worked at GPO as a printer/proofreader in the 1970s before leaving to serve in various elected posts within the International Typographical Union, which later merged with the Communications Workers of America, where he rose to become Senior Vice President and President of the Printing, Publishing, and Media Workers Sector. Hearings were held before the Senate Rules and Administration Committee in May 2010 and in July the nomination was reported favorably to the full Senate, where it remained pending on the Senate executive calendar until the close of the session. President Obama made a recess appointment on December 29, 2010. Boarman was sworn in as the 26th Public Printer on January 3, 2011. The President resubmitted the nomination in the 112th Congress, where it was reported favorably by the Senate Rules and Administration Committee on May 11, 2011.

William J. Boarman was appointed by President Obama as the 26th Public Printer in December 2010.

With Federal spending and efforts to control the Federal deficit dominating the agenda in the early months of the 112th Congress, Public Printer Boarman imposed changes to cut costs and rein in GPO's spending, particularly in overhead areas. He cut GPO's annual spending plan for FY 2011, reduced GPO's appropriations request for fiscal year 2012, realigned management to have the Chief Financial Officer reporting directly to him, and implemented a task force to recover outstanding payments,

Public Printer Boarman, Archivist David Ferriero, GPO Chief of Staff Vance-Cooks, and officials of the Office of the Federal Register present President Barack Obama with the first volume of his Public Papers in early 2011.

known as "chargebacks," from Federal agencies. He began a series of meetings with Senators and Representatives on GPO's oversight and appropriations committees to discuss Congress's information product needs and issued an online survey of congressional offices on their continued need for print copies of the *Congressional Record*, the *Federal Register*, and other publications. GPO launched its page on Facebook, implemented a project to make Federal court opinions publicly available online, and worked with the General Services Administration to make 100 consumer-oriented publications available to the public via GPO's partnership with Google Books. In February 2011, Public Printer Boarman and GPO's Chief of Staff Davita Vance-Cooks visited President Obama in the Oval Office to join in the presentation of the first bound volume of the President's Public Papers.

At his public swearing-in ceremony held in January, Public Printer Boarman said, "Keeping America informed is a function rooted in the Constitution, and it's one of the great national purposes served by this agency." In his closing words, he also remarked on Beatrice Warde's poem, observing:

> For us at the GPO, Beatrice Ward's poem is about a valued and special place where the official, authenticated word of our Congress and our constitutional government is reproduced and disseminated for the people of our great Nation. We still print—using processes that are thoroughly computerized—but we also use digital technology in new and exciting ways. The forms and capabilities of that technology continue to grow, and we embrace them to carry out our job. …

> But we never forget that the principles of our work are enshrined in Warde's poem, and whether what we do is in print or in bits and bytes, and whether in the long run we call it a printing office or an information office, we never forget that we stand on sacred ground, and that we are here to serve. ❧

The GPO story is one of men and women using changing technologies to compose, print, bind, index, catalog, and distribute. Technological development and advance have been constant themes from that first March day in 1861. A history of GPO is a record of not only of what GPO did over years and the people who performed that work, but the technology they used to do the job.

In 1861, lead type was set by hand by skilled compositors. Forms of made-up pages were placed directly on the presses. GPO was probably still using hand presses in 1861, but was certainly using steam-driven cylinder presses that moved the paper mechanically, which had been perfected a decade or so earlier. Paper in large sheets was dampened and fed into the press by pressmen (and women) who in turn took finished sheets off. Printing on the second side required that the paper be turned and fed again, until the introduction of the perfecting press, which printed on both sides of the sheet. Printed sheets were dried under great weight, then cut, collated, and bound.

By 1875, type was still set by hand, but rather than being always mounted directly on the press, stereotype plates were cast from it and mounted on the press. Some presses used a continuous roll (or web) of paper, although sheet feeding was still common. Paper was no longer dampened, and a wide variety of sophisticated machines cut, collated, and bound sheets into books, pamphlets, and other products. This period saw the development of machines that stitched or sewed along the folded edge of the sheets to create multileaf pamphlets.

Throughout these early years, there were continuing improvements in press capability and speed, but the slowness of hand-set type meant that GPO could not take full advantage of their efficiency. That changed in 1904, when the agency began to use Monotype and Linotype machines to set type. Within a few years GPO had the largest battery in the world of both common kinds of machines. Pages composed on Monotype or Linotype were cast into plates for use on ever-larger and faster presses. Typesetting machines were capable of setting lines of type per minute,

compared with minutes per line of hand-set type, and in this period composition was finally able to keep pace with fast, efficient presses. Coupled with improvements in paper-making, these new production efficiencies rippled throughout the printing industry and GPO, driving down the cost of printing and leading to an explosion of printed matter. These developments resulted in higher literacy rates nationwide and—where GPO was concerned—in a new ability of the Government and the public to interact through the printed word.

In the years immediately after 1925, GPO began to supplement its letterpress production, in which type or plates directly touched each sheet, with offset printing, a lithographic process invented in 1901 by Ira W. Rubel, in which printing plates are created from photographic negatives. Offset plates transfer an image from the plate to a rubber blanket which, in turn, transfers it to the paper. The offset process was designed to yield longer print runs more economically, with the "offset" transfer of the image to the blanket to the paper lasting longer than raised type, which would eventually wear down. Type was set with Monotype and Linotype machines and negatives were created by photographing made-up pages. After World War II, offset printing superseded letterpress at GPO except in the production of the daily *Congressional Record* and *Federal Register*, which continued to use a modified letterpress process utilizing photopolymer plates until the acquisition of new offset presses in 1995.

In the 1950s, building on the capabilities introduced with offset printing, GPO began using typesetting machines that produced photographic images or negatives rather than metal type. Although these machines never superseded hot metal typesetting, they were the precursor of the technology that would. In 1967, CBS Laboratories, the Mergenthaler Co., and GPO introduced the Linotron, a machine to produce page negatives from magnetic tape input. The Linotron was GPO's entrance into the age of computerized typesetting.

By 1975, the descendants of the Linotron had begun to close out the use of hot metal composition at GPO with the transition to the electronic photocomposition process, and by 1985 the end of hot metal typesetting was over. GPO's electronic composition systems, including an automated composition system developed at the agency specifically for the production of congressional and *Federal Register* work, called Microcomp, still produced a photographic negative that was used to create an offset plate. In the 1990s, systems came into use that produced printing plates directly from digital files. This direct-to-plate technology rapidly replaced earlier photographic methods and coincided with the move, inside GPO and among the users it serves, to disseminate and use information online as well as in print. GPO launched *GPO Access* in 1994 to make a variety of congressional and other agency publications available over the Internet.

The digital transformation of GPO over the past generation has yielded significant savings to the taxpayers. Since GPO first began computerizing its prepress functions in the 1970s, the agency's use of digital information technology has generated productivity improvements that have reduced the cost of congressional information products by more than two-thirds in real economic terms, resulting in cumulative savings in the hundreds of millions of dollars. GPO has had similar success in reducing the cost of information dissemination to the public while expanding the availability of Government information products and public access.

The opening of the 112th Congress was dominated by the issue of reducing Federal spending to bring the growing deficit under control. GPO was not immune from this effort, along with other agencies sustaining a significant funding cut in the final funding bill for fiscal year 2011 and facing potential additional cuts in fiscal year 2012. At this writing, legislation has been introduced to reduce the print production of the congressional bills and the *Congressional Record* and to achieve other savings through the reduction of Federal printing overall. At the same time,

GPO's digital work continues to grow, with new calls for online support for the Constitutional Authority Statements now required of all legislation in the House of Representatives, growing demand by Federal agencies for secure identification credentials featuring computer chips, digitization of previously printed documents such as all issues of the *Congressional Record* dating to 1873 in collaboration with the Library of Congress, a new partnership with the Administrative Office of the U.S. Courts to publish selected court information online, and continued development of GPO's Web presence in FDsys.

On GPO's 150th anniversary, Representative Robert A. Brady (PA) delivered remarks in the *Congressional Record* offering congratulations and best wishes to the agency. Noting that he represented Philadelphia, the home of Benjamin Franklin and the seat of the Constitutional Convention at which the Founding Fathers enshrined the requirement that Congress publish its proceedings, Rep. Brady said:

> In a day when we are working hard to cut costs and improve services, the GPO provides a model of how an agency with a history of taking advantage of technological change has used that capability to generate lasting savings while expanding services to Congress, Federal agencies, and the public. The dedicated men and women of GPO have resorted continually to technology improvements to perform their work more efficiently, at one time using ink on paper to set the text for the Emancipation Proclamation, and today—as another President from Illinois leads the Nation—using e-Books, digital databases, and other new and emerging applications to achieve its founding mission of *Keeping America Informed*. ❧

HEADS OF PUBLIC PRINTING | 1861 – 2011

GPO Superintendents of Public Printing

JOHN D. DEFREES, March 23, 1861 – August 31, 1866

CORNELIUS WENDELL, September 1, 1866 – February 28, 1867

JOHN D. DEFREES, March 1, 1867 – April 14, 1869

Congressional Printer

ALMON W. CLAPP, April 15, 1869 – July 31, 1876

Public Printers

ALMON W. CLAPP, August 1, 1876 – May 30, 1877

JOHN D. DeFREES, June 1, 1877 – April 14, 1882

STERLING P. ROUNDS, April 15, 1882 – September 12, 1886

THOMAS BENEDICT, September 13, 1886 – May 6, 1889

FRANK W. PALMER, May 7, 1889 – May 2, 1894

THOMAS BENEDICT, May 3, 1894 – March 30, 1897

FRANK W. PALMER, March 31, 1897 – September 8, 1905

O. J. RICKETTS (Acting), September 9, 1905 – November 27, 1905

CHARLES A. STILLINGS, November 28, 1905 – February 5, 1908

WILLIAM S. ROSSITER (Acting), February 6, 1908 – June 7, 1908

CAPT. HENRY T. BRIAN (Acting), June 8, 1908

JOHN S. LEECH, June 9, 1908 – November 30, 1908

SAMUEL B. DONNELLY, December 1, 1908 – June 20, 1913

CORNELIUS FORD, June 20, 1913 – April 4, 1921

GEORGE H. CARTER, April 5, 1921 – July 1, 1934

AUGUSTUS E. GIEGENGACK, July 2, 1934 – March 15, 1948

JOHN J. DEVINY (Acting), March 16, 1948 – May 5, 1948

JOHN J. DEVINY, May 6, 1948 – February 28, 1953

PHILIP L. COLE (Acting), March 1, 1953 – April 27, 1953

RAYMOND BLATTENBERGER, April 28, 1953 – January 31, 1961

JOHN M. WILSON (Acting), February 1, 1961 – March 4, 1961

FELIX M. CRISTOFANE (Acting), March 7, 1961 – March 17, 1961

JAMES L. HARRISON, March 17, 1961 – March 31, 1970

ADOLPHUS NICHOLS SPENCE II, April 1, 1970 – January 11, 1972

HARRY L. HUMPHREY (Acting), January 11, 1972 – January 31, 1973

LEONARD GOLDEN (Acting), February 1, 1973 – February 28, 1973

THOMAS F. McCORMICK, March 1, 1973 – November 1, 1977

JOHN J. BOYLE, November 1, 1977 – February 29, 1980

SAMUEL L. SAYLOR (Acting), March 3, 1980 – August 4, 1981

DANFORD L. SAWYER, Jr., August 5, 1981 – January 27, 1984

WILLIAM J. BARRETT (Acting), January 28, 1984 – December 11, 1984

RALPH E. KENNICKELL, Jr., December 11, 1984 – November 18, 1988

JOSEPH E. JENIFER (Acting), November 19, 1988 – March 7, 1990

ROBERT W. HOUK, March 8, 1990 – February 19, 1993

MICHAEL F. DIMARIO (Acting), February 19, 1993 – November 8, 1993

MICHAEL F. DIMARIO, November 9, 1993 – November 20, 2002

BRUCE R. JAMES, November 20, 2002 – December 31, 2006

WILLIAM H. TURRI (Acting), January 1, 2007 – October 10, 2007

ROBERT C. TAPELLA, October 10, 2007 – December 28, 2010

PAUL ERICKSON (Acting) December 29, 2010 – January 3, 2011

WILLIAM J. BOARMAN, January 3, 2011 –

1   Beatrice L. Warde, *Bombed But Unbeaten* (New York: The Typophiles, 1941).

2   Ibid.

3   Harold C. Relyea, *Title 44, Public Printing and Documents, A Brief Historical Overview,* Congressional Research Service Issue Brief 79–36 GOV (Washington: Congressional Research Service, 1979).

4   The original Government Document No. 1 is housed in the Library Company of Philadelphia. See the exhibition catalog, *A Rising People: The Founding of the United States 1765 to 1789* (Philadelphia: The American Philosophical Society, 1976), p. 47.

5   David Mitchell Ivester, "The Constitutional Right to Know," *Hastings Constitutional Law Quarterly 4* (Winter, 1977), pp. 109–163.

6   Ibid.

7   Quoted in *Report of the Serial Set Study Group* (Washington, DC: Government Printing Office, 1994), p. 4.

8   George Barnum and August M. Imholtz, " 'Hidden Gem' In Senate Report," *Unum: Newsletter of the Office of the Secretary of the Senate 8/4* (Winter 2004), p. 2.

9   Relyea, 1979, p. 8.

10   Laurence Schmeckebeier, *The Government Printing Office, Its History, Activities, and Organization* (Baltimore: Johns Hopkins University Press, 1925), pp. 3–4.

11   Article in an issue of *The Printer* (unknown place of publication, ca. 1859), of which GPO has proof sheets in its collection.

12   John B. Ellis, *Sights and Secrets of the National Capital: A Work Descriptive of Washington City* (NewYork: United States Publishing Company, 1869).

13   Kathleen McKirchy, *America's Oldest Union: The Columbia Typographical Union 101* (Washington, DC: Columbia Typographical Union, 1990).

14   John Hope Franklin, *The Emancipation Proclamation* (New York: Doubleday, 1963), p. 58.

15   Library of Congress Web site, http://memory.loc.gov/ammem/alhtml/alrb/step/09221862/001.html, accessed 11/10/2010.

16   John D. Defrees to John G. Nicolay, Wednesday, December 17, 1862 (Emancipation Proclamation), Library of Congress Web site, http://memory.loc.gov/cgi-bin/query/r?ammem/mal:@field(DOCID+@lit(d4243200)), accessed 11/18/09.

17   Robert E. Kling, Jr., *The Government Printing Office* (New York: Praeger Publishers, 1970), pp.110–111.

18   Relyea, 1979, pp. 11–12.

19   J. A. Huston. *Historical Sketch of the Government Printing Office, 1861–1916* (Washington: The Fortson Press, 1916), p. 51.

20   Michael E. Grass, "Jefferson's Bible Returns, Controversial as Ever," *Roll Call*, January 20, 2005; Richard N. Ostling, "Patchwork Bible Provides Look as Jefferson's World," AP, printed in the *Washington Post*, August 21, 2001.

21   Willard B. Gatewood, Jr., *Theodore Roosevelt and the Art of Controversy: Episodes of the White House Years* (Baton Rouge: Louisiana State University Press, 1970), pp. 169–172.

22   Rossiter Commission report (1908), summarized in *100 GPO Years* (Washington, DC: GPO, 1961), p. 90.

23   See John Walters, "Politics as Usual: the Joint Committee on Printing and Executive Agency Publishing, 1919–1921," *Government Publications Review* 20 (1993), pp. 41-59; also, "Wilson Rebukes Congress in Veto as Trying to Muzzle," *New York Times*, May 14, 1920.

24   Kling, 1970, p. 41.

25   Geoffrey T. Hellman, "Profiles—Mr. Public Printer-II," *The New Yorker*, June 19, 1943, p. 30.

26   James M. Goode, *Outdoor Sculpture of Washington D.C.: A Comprehensive Historical Guide* (Washington, DC: Smithsonian Press, 1974).

27   For a history of the *Federal Register*, see Relyea, 1979, pp. 29–35, and "The Federal Register: Origins, Formulation, Realization, and Heritage, prepared remarks delivered at the National Archives and Records Administration for the 75th Anniversary of the Federal Register, September 15, 2010, Washington, DC.

28   *Public Papers of the Presidents of the United States, President Harry S. Truman*, v. 5, 1949 (Washington, DC: GPO, 1960), pp. 346–347.

29   See *Executive Sessions of the Senate Permanent Subcommittee on Investigations of the Committee on Government Operations, 83rd Congress, Second Session, 1953*. Made public January, 2003. Senate Print 107–84 (Washington, DC: GPO, 2003). See also newspaper articles appearing daily between August 11, 1953, and August 30, 1953, in *The Washington Post, The Washington Star, The Washington Daily News*, and the Washington *Times-Herald*.

30   Kling, 1970, pp. 116–117, 151–153.

31   Kling, 1970, pp. 187–197.

32   Congress of the United States, Joint Committee on Printing, Fact Finding Hearing In Re: Joint Bargaining Committee on Unions, GPO, and the International Association of Machinists Franklin Lodge 2135 and GPO, Hearings Held Before Frederick U. Reel, July and August 1982, pp. 11–12.

33   Office of Technology Assessment, *Informing the Nation: Federal Information Dissemination in the Electronic Era* (Washington, DC: GPO, 1987).

34   *Government Printing Office: Monopoly-like Status Contributes to Inefficiency and Ineffectiveness*, GGD–90–107 (Washington, DC: General Accounting Office, 1990).

35   Vice President Al Gore, *From Red Tape to Results, Creating a Government The Works Better and Costs Less: Report of the National Performance Review* (Washington: GPO, 1993).

36   Harold C. Relyea, *Public Printing Reform: Issues and Actions*, CRS Issue Brief 98–687 GOV (Washington, DC: Congressional Research Service, 2003), p. 10.

37   "GPO Touts the Good Business of Green Efforts," *Roll Call*, November 17, 2010.

38   *Government Printing Office: Issues Faced in Obtaining a New Facility*, GAO–09–392R, February 20, 2009 (Washington, DC: Government Accountability Office, 2009).

Along with the annual reports of the Public Printers, for the pre-1960 period the best known history, recently reissued with an index, is *100 GPO Years 1861–1961* (Washington, DC: GPO, 1961), prepared under the direction of Public Printer James L. Harrison. *100 GPO Years* followed R.W. Kerr's *History of the Government Printing Office (at Washington, D.C.), with a brief record of the Public Printing for a Century, 1789–1881* (Lancaster, PA: Inquirer Printing and Publishing Co., 1881); J. A. Huston's *Historical Sketch of the Government Printing Office 1861–1916* (Washington, DC: The Fortson Press, 1916); and Laurence F. Schmeckebier's *The Government Printing Office: Its History, Activities, and Organization* (Baltimore: The Johns Hopkins Press, 1925). Robert L. Kling, a GPO official, published *The Government Printing Office* (New York: Praeger Publishers, 1970), as part of the *Praeger Library of U.S. Government Departments and Agencies*, which provided a comprehensive review of Federal printing and GPO from the colonial period to 1970, drawing on most of the earlier GPO histories. A noteworthy article on Public Printer Giegengack was a three-part profile by Geoffrey T. Hellman which appeared in *The New Yorker* June 12, 19, and 26, 1943, under the title "Mr. Public Printer." The account of the post-1960 period relies on a variety of sources. There have been articles written by GPO historians Daniel McGilvray and James Cameron published in GPO's newsletter, *Typeline*. The McGilvray articles appeared during the observance of GPO's 125th anniversary in 1986 and are available today on GPO's Web site, while several of the Cameron articles have been edited for inclusion in this book.

In 1979, *Title 44, United States Code—Public Printing and Documents: A Brief Historical Overview* was prepared as a Congressional Research Service issue brief by Harold C. Relyea (CRS Report No. 79–36 GOV, February 23, 1979). In more recent years, Relyea also prepared updates on GPO in, for example, *Public Printing Reform: Issues and Actions* (CRS Report for Congress, Order Code 98–687 GOV, June 17, 2003), and he recently wrote a history of the *Federal Register*, which will appear as "The *Federal Register*: Origins, Formulation, Realization, and Heritage" in an upcoming issue of *Government Information Quarterly*.

Unreported in *100 GPO Years* was the extensive investigation of GPO conducted in the summer of 1953 by the Senate Permanent Subcommittee on Investigations of the Committee on Government Operations, led by Senator Joseph McCarthy. Though described in press accounts of the time in the *Washington Star* and the *Washington Post*, among other newspapers, the full extent of the investigation, major parts of which were conducted in executive session, were not made public until January 2003, when the full hearings were published in Senate Committee on Governmental Affairs, *Executive Sessions of the Senate Permanent Subcommittee on Investigations of the Committee on Government Operations*, Eighty-third Congress, First Session, 1953, Made Public January 2003 (Washington, DC: GPO, 2003; vol. 2). Other key Government reports include Joint Committee on Printing, "Federal Government Printing and Publishing: Policy Issues," Report of the Ad Hoc Advisory Committee on Revision of Title 44 to the Joint Committee on Printing, Committee Print (Washington, DC: GPO, 1979); and several by the former Office of Technology Assessment, particularly the OTA's singular *Informing the Nation: Federal Information Dissemination in an Electronic Age* (Washington, DC: GPO, 1988).

In addition to various audit reports on GPO issued over the years by the Government Accountability Office, as it is now known, at least two substantial management reviews of GPO have been performed in recent decades, including Joint Committee on Printing, "Analysis and Evaluation of Selected Government Printing Office Operations, Prepared by Coopers and Lybrand, an Independent Consulting Firm, Washington, D.C." (Washington, DC: GPO, 1979), and Booz-Allen & Hamilton, "Management Audit of the Government Printing Office, Final Report May 21, 1998" Submitted to General Accounting Office, General Accounting Division (Washington, DC: GAO, 1998).

A number of legislative histories are available for the substantive legislation affecting GPO. Through the early 1980s, these actions are collected in the multi-volume set *GPO, Office of the General Counsel, Legislative Histories of the Laws Affecting the U.S. Government Printing*

Office, as Codified in Title 44 of the U.S. Code (Washington, DC: GPO, 1983). Many of these documents can also be found in various issues of the *U.S. Code Congressional and Administrative News*. In 1979–80, 1989–90, and again in 1997–98, GPO was involved in major proposals to overhaul Title 44, during hearings and subsequent legislative consideration of H.R. 5424—the National Publications Act—in the 96th Congress, H.R. 3890, in the 101st Congress, and S. 2288—the Wendell H. Ford Government Publications Act—in the 105th Congress.

Documents related to the Supreme Court's decision in *INS* v. *Chadha*, 462 U.S. 919 (1983), include memoranda issued by the Justice Department's Office of Legal Counsel (Memorandum for William H. Taft, IV, Deputy Secretary of Defense, Department of Defense, from Theodore B. Olson, Assistant Attorney General, Office of Legal Counsel, Re: Effect of *INS* v. *Chadha* on 44 U.S.C. 501, Public Printing and Documents, March 2, 1984; Memorandum for Michael J. Horowitz, Counsel to the Director, Office of Management and Budget (OMB), from Theodore B. Olson, Assistant Attorney General, Office of Legal Counsel, Re: Constitutionality of Proposed Regulations of Joint Committee on Printing under *Buckley* v. *Valeo* and *INS* v. *Chadha*, April 11, 1984; Memorandum for Michael J. Horowitz, Counsel to the Director, OMB, from Theodore B. Olson, Assistant Attorney General, Office of Legal Counsel, Re: Government Printing, Binding, and Distribution Policies and Guidelines of the Joint Committee on Printing, August 21, 1984; and Memorandum for Emily C. Hewitt, General Counsel, General Services Administration, from Walter Dellinger, Assistant Attorney General, Office of Legal Counsel, Re: Government Printing Office Involvement in Executive Branch Printing, May 31, 1996). Associated documents include Federal Acquisition Circular (FAC) 84–25, published in the *Federal Register* on March 20, 1987; and Office of Management and Budget, Procurement of Printing and Duplicating through the Government Printing Office, Memorandum M–02–07, from Mitchell E. Daniels, Jr., Director, OMB, to Heads of Executive Departments and Agencies (May 3, 2002).

Two court cases with major implications for GPO and its employees were the *Thompson* and *McKenzie* cases, decided in the U.S. District Court for the District of Columbia. Another prominent case was *Lewis* v. *Sawyer*, U.S. District Court for the District of Columbia, and upheld on appeal (1983), which held the Public Printer is accountable to the direction of the Joint Committee on Printing as the GPO's Board of Directors. Another case left undiscussed in this book was *Doe* v. *McMillan*, 412 U.S. 306, in which the Supreme Court held, among other things, that the Public Printer and the Superintendent of Documents are protected by the doctrine of official immunity for information printed in congressional documents.

There is a wealth of discussion of the Depository Library Program in journals such as *Government Publications Review* and *Government Information Quarterly*. Clare Beck discusses the early days of the Public Documents Division in her biography of GPO's first librarian *The New Woman as Librarian: The Career of Adelaide Hasse* (Lanham, MD: Scarecrow Press, 2006)

Other key sources used for this volume were GPO's congressional appropriations hearings; GPO annual reports and related data, including supplemental data published annually as "United States Government Printing Office Statistics" (GPO Publication 410.2); various GPO strategic plans, including the 1990 issue of *GPO/2001: Vision for a New Millenium* and the *2004 Strategic Vision for the 21st Century*; issues of GPO's internal employee newsletter, the *Typeline*, dating to the 1960s; various press accounts of GPO; as well as scholarly articles about GPO in such publications as the *Journal of Government Information*, *Government Information Quarterly*, *Documents To The People*, *Printing History*, and other journals. All photographs are from GPO's collection, unless noted in the caption.

As important as any of these sources have been the memories of GPO employees who have contributed to the production of this volume, and their willingness to share them. ❧

ACKNOWLEDGEMENTS

The writing of *Keeping America Informed* began in 2010, based initially on a series of articles prepared by former GPO historian Daniel MacGilvray for GPO's 125th anniversary in 1986. Most of them first appeared in GPO's in-house newsletter *Typeline*. The present authors have used that short history as a foundation and guide throughout. Another former GPO historian, James T. Cameron, authored a series of features on GPO's history in past issues of *Typeline* that have become many of the sidebar features in this book. Jim has been a source of wise advice and skillful editing for this new volume.

Several individuals have read and commented on the text with great thoughtfulness and candor. Former Public Printers Michael F. DiMario and Robert C. Tapella each made suggestions that improved the book. GPO was extremely fortunate to have Senate Historian Donald Ritchie, Congressional Research Service (CRS) Specialist in American National Government R. Eric Peterson, and retired CRS Specialist in American National Government Harold C. Relyea all review and comment on the draft. Retired GPO Library Programs Service Director Gil Baldwin and Bonnie Baldwin, both professional librarians, reviewed the text, as did retired GPO Congressional Relations Officer C. Michael Bright. The draft was also reviewed by Fred Jordan, freelance writer and editor.

The Honorable David S. Ferriero, Archivist of the United States, provided a digitized text of the original resolution establishing GPO, and Christina R. Smith of the National Archives and Records Administration gave useful advice. Thanks go to the staff of the Joint Committee on Printing of the 111th Congress, the U.S. Senate Library, the U.S. Senate Historical Office, and the U.S. Senate Curator's Office for their support and guidance.

Ten Federal depository libraries and librarians have generously lent materials for the preparation of the 2011 exhibit at GPO that complements this book: Denison University, Granville, OH, Mary Webb Prophet; Indiana University, Bloomington, IN, Lou Malcomb; Ohio University, Athens, OH, Doreen Hockenberry; University of Maryland College of Law, Baltimore, MD, William Sleeman; University of North Texas, Denton, TX, Starr Hoffman; Louisville Free Public Library, Louisville, KY, Claudia Fitch; Jackson District Library, Jackson, MI, Nadia ElAnanni; Wyoming State Law Library, Cheyenne, WY, Kathy Carlson; Southeastern Louisiana University, Hammond, LA, Lori Smith; and Oklahoma State University, Stillwater, OK, John Phillips. Suzanne Campbell, GPO's law librarian, also provided documents, assistance, and support.

Nora A. Bailey, Esq., and Roderic V.O. Boggs, Esq., provided information on plaintiffs in race- and gender-discrimination suits against GPO. Clare Beck, author of an authoritative biography of Adelaide Hasse, provided invaluable information about GPO's first librarian and her co-workers.

Finally, GPO's proofreading section and foreperson M. Michael Abramson, deserve special recognition for their skill, diligence, and expertise. GPO's Brand Manager, Dean A. Gardei, created a design for the book that balances the written word with the photographs.

The Photographs

Most of the photographs in this history are from GPO's own photo collection and many are published here for the first time. In the few cases in which a photo or image has come from another source, acknowledgement is given in the caption.

COLOPHON

The text for *Keeping America Informed* is set in Granjon, a typeface designed in 1924 for the Linotype & Machinery Co., Ltd., by George William Jones. It is based on a font designed by Jean Jannon (c. 1615) derived from designs by Claude Garamond (c. 1480-1561). Revivals based on what type scholar Beatrice Warde terms "one special Roman and italic owned by the Imprimerie Nationale, Paris" became popular in the early 20th century. Granjon is referred to by Warde as "…the first and immeasurably the best of the modern revivals." Granjon was first used by GPO on *The Writings of George Washington* (1931) and the type's designer commented that "such beautiful work…will exert a big influence on American printing." Granjon was among GPO's standard fonts throughout the era of hot metal composition.

The text is set in Adobe (r) Granjon, a digital font based on the Linotype original, with headings in Adobe (r) Trajan, a modern all-capitals display font designed by Carol Twombly, and printed using vegetable oil-based inks. The text is printed on coated offset book paper containing 10% postconsumer recycled fiber, produced utilizing a chlorine-free process for enhanced permanence. The cover is printed on uncoated cover stock containing 30% postconsumer recycled fiber. Both papers carry nationally and internationally-recognized chain-of-custody certifications.